Steps to Singing for Voice Classes

Third Edition

Royal Stanton

late of De Anza College

**WAVELAND
PRESS, INC.**

Long Grove, Illinois

D0323291

* 000218213 *

For Marcia, Lynne, Jackie, and Patti

For information about this book, contact:
Waveland Press, Inc.
4180 IL Route 83, Suite 101
Long Grove, IL 60047-9580
(847) 634-0081
info@waveland.com
www.waveland.com

CONTENTS

STEP 9   MOVING TOWARD ARTISTRY   137

SONG COLLECTION

Rounds

PREFACE FOR THE INSTRUCTOR

OBJECTIVES OF THIS BOOK

This book is designed to help you teach classes of beginners in singing.

It offers a structure of information and organized activity on which you can base your teaching. It contains materials and procedures that have proven their effectiveness in the author's thirty years of voice class teaching at the community college level. The book puts at your disposal a ready-made, proven durable format with which to begin. It is carefully constructed so that it may be used "as is" or enriched by the addition of your own methods and materials, which you feel are especially suited to the classes you teach. It cannot provide, or replace, the individual guidance and personal attention you give to your students. It cannot supply specific remedies for every vocal problem they bring to class. In such matters they must rely on your personal involvement and professional experience.

The text of the book is addressed directly to *beginning* singers. It assumes that the majority of them are to some extent musical or vocal laypersons who are venturing into the organized process of singing as relative newcomers. To engage and hold their interest, technical matters are explained in the most forthright, untechnical language possible. The entire text of this third edition has been rewritten with a view to presenting each successive step in the training process in a manner that beginners will readily understand, trying to anticipate their questions and frustrations, as well as their lay view of the particular challenges involved. Throughout, suggestions are made for *explicit things to do,* in the firm belief that, since singing is a "doing" activity, insights will result most readily from actually producing sounds with the voice. This direct approach to the student is not an attempt to bypass your teaching but rather is aimed at getting students involved and asking questions that you are there to answer, thus providing one of your best opportunities for effective teaching.

Because it emphasizes steps for beginners, the book does not attempt to be an exhaustive course in voice training, from first vocalise to final professional contract. The aim here is to guide beginners from their initial tentative approaches to phonation to the outer edges of performance and the rudiments of interpretation, to an extent that allows them to see that singing *does* involve songs, performance, and expression—as they undoubtedly expected it to—and is not merely a receding horizon of endless exercises and technical devices. Nevertheless, the book makes no attempt to delve deeply into interpretation, styling, repertoire, and the subtleties of individual expression. These are realms for which private coaching must be obtained.

ORGANIZATION OF THE BOOK

The Steps

To present a logical arrangement of the materials of voice training, a plan of nine successive steps was evolved. The exact order of these steps is not as important as its concept of building one achievement on another. The book avoids adherence to any "school" of voice training but rather is concerned with concepts that are widely accepted as important components of beginning training. These components constitute the nine steps. They begin with preparatory attitudes and understandings needed for singing, and proceed to posture and breathing requirements, the production of tone, the control of vowels and consonants, the demands of placement, legato technique and phrasing, concepts of performance, the need for musicianship, and the fundamentals of expressive singing.

If your personal philosophy of voice training favors a different order of subjects, you are encouraged to restructure the steps according to your experience. Such a restructuring could well be the most effective means available to motivate a particular class.

The Lessons

Every step is divided into short lessons designed to fit a standard class hour, or in some cases a short sequence of hours. Each lesson focuses on one important concept of singing, and includes: a statement of the concept in direct, understandable language; suggested class activities illustrating what has been explained; exercise materials or other means of practicing what has been learned; and informal activities suggested for the student to use (On Your Own) for further exploration of the ideas presented. The aim has been to supply alternative activities in most lessons—more than would be needed in any given situation—in recognition of the fact that a particular approach may be unsuitable or impractical for a given class. You are encouraged to pick and choose, to alter and augment the lesson with materials of your own selection. Users of this book in various regions of the country have stressed the value of this diversity.

In the *bel canto* tradition, years of technical preparation were required before a student was thought ready to sing the first song. Modern, media-conditioned beginners, in contrast, may come to class hoping to dispense with technical exercises altogether, intent on improving their voices by "expressing themselves" through singing familiar songs. They need to be shown that such aspirations will almost certainly be frustrated by their limited technical skills and that disciplines other than expression—such nitty-gritty as posture, breathing, tone, and diction—must be mastered first if expression is to have meaning. To help make this view more attractive, the book suggests a middle ground between exercise singing and song singing, one that not only draws on the evident satisfactions of singing enjoyable and melodious songs within the beginner's capabilities but also makes clear the genuine pleasure of producing consistent, resonant, and deeply supported tone for its own sake, through the use of interesting and challenging exercises.

Materials for Developing Singers' Musicianship

Throughout the book the singer's fundamental need for musicianship is stressed. Materials are provided that will allow you to coordinate such an emphasis with the purely vocal instruction that will be the principal focus of your class activities. Step 7, Learning Musicianship, places the concept of musicianly singing directly in the ordered sequence of steps to successful singing, which is the framework of the book. In addition, more detailed materials for class assignments or individual work are supplied in Appendix 3, Musicianship Information for Singers. This appendix, written in terms of what the *singer* needs to know, provides basic information about the score, staffs and notation, rhythm, intervals, scales, keys and key signatures, and expressive markings. How (or whether) this material is used in your class is left to your discretion. It has proven valuable for many class situations in which earlier editions of this book have been used.

Other optional instructional aids are provided in Appendixes 1 and 2. Appendix 1 lists Seven Steps to Learning a New Song, providing an ordered sequence of steps for the beginner in learning the unfamiliar songs assigned in this class. Appendix 2 provides a sample evaluation form for class, recital, and individual use, in the event that you find such evaluation procedures to be productive methods of vocal instruction. The materials of both of these appendixes were developed in extensive classroom use, and have demonstrated their value.

The Song Collection

Three groups of songs have been included in the Song Collection. The first, Concert Songs, draws on standard repertoire from various centuries and styles to supply a group of pieces within beginners' capabilities that have proven durable and interesting. They have been selected strictly because they have demonstrated lasting musical value and attractiveness. Considerations of status, popularity, originality, variety of style, suitability for recital programming, or composer reputation have had little influence in the selection. Simple, singable melodies without excessive vocal or musical demands have been favored, since beginners can most readily master the basics of breathing, tone production, diction, and phrasing if they are not confronted with great difficulty at the outset. Most of these songs will be unfamiliar to the beginner, which is probably an advantage. When singers approach a song whose image has not previously been colored by another singer's "expressive" performance on a recording, radio, or television, they do not have to unlearn borrowed concepts before they can begin to discover what their own voices can do with the song.

A group of Folksongs from various traditions and cultures has been included because of their proven durability and singability and because they are more familiar than the Concert Songs. Having familiar materials at hand has proven valuable for illustrating a point quickly with a song—perhaps used as an exercise—that does not need a long preparation time.

Several pieces in both the Concert Songs and Folksongs are printed in more than one key for convenience. In addition, a group of familiar Rounds has been added. These have proven valuable in class use, particularly in encouraging timid singers to join freely in using their voices under the comforting shelter of group singing. These rounds are familiar and fun to sing, and at the outset can stimulate the attitude that singing is enjoyable. There can be no better starting place for vocal instruction.

Lists of songs, recordings, and books have been omitted purposely, in order not to make the book cumbersome through overstructuring. Such lists tend to become outdated with remarkable speed; recordings available as this is being written may well be out of print by the time the third edition is printed. Suggestions made to the author and publisher from various regions of the United States reveal that what would be usable or desirable in one area might be considered wholly unsuitable in another. In this matter you are the expert-in-residence with the needed knowledge of appropriate materials. Your personal perception of what recordings are available and relevant, what songs will best serve your class, and what library resources are available will provide far more productive guidance for your students than arbitrary lists made up at a distance.

ADVANTAGES OF THE CLASS METHOD OF TEACHING VOICE

While this book strongly urges students who are seriously interested in genuine vocal accomplishment to begin private voice coaching as soon as possible, it is written in the firm conviction that class voice training has distinct advantages for the beginner. The congenial social atmosphere of a well-run class can bolster students' timorous courage and give them a chance to overcome self-consciousness in a realistic setting. Hearing classmates struggle with similar vocal problems gives students an invaluable perspective on their own efforts. What is most important, learning the joys of controlled singing in a friendly environment encourages beginners to think of singing as a natural, peer-approved activity, not simply as something difficult or technical in which only odd or peculiarly talented types engage.

This is particularly important because most of the beginners to whom this book is addressed have little intention of pursuing vocal training to a professional or artistic level of accomplishment. They come to this class because of their budding interest in singing as a pleasurable activity, hoping that they will be shown practical, interesting ways of improving their voices in order to enhance that interest. They may tend to be wary of the exacting disciplines expected of the professional singer, seeing serious voice training as a series of forbidding or boring technicalities whose relevance to their personal aims is not quite clear. This book tries to present the class setting as an attractive milieu in which they may discover what their voices can do and what might be expected at more advanced levels of training and performance.

The author expresses his sincere appreciation to: Le Grande Anderson, Fresno City College; Margery Anwyl, University of California, Santa Barbara; Susan Burns, California State Polytechnic University, Pomona; Diane Davidson, Los Angeles Valley College; John Dietz, Indiana University of Pennsylvania; Mary Ann Dutton, Glendale Community College; Sue Harmon, California State University, Fullerton; Mary Moore, Mount San Antonio College; June Swartwout, West Virginia University; Lee Vail, California State University, Long Beach; and Robert Waterstripe, Edinboro State College, for assistance provided in their manuscript reviews and helpful critical suggestions. He is also particularly—and admiringly—indebted to editors Sheryl Fullerton and Judith McKibben for their patience and expertise, which have been so crucial in bringing this third edition to completion.

Making Preparations

Your first step toward successful singing is to be sure that you understand the basic mental and physical conditions that make singing possible. Before we begin systematic examination of the singing process itself, you need to be aware of concepts that make the process work.

Since the *physical* act of singing begins with breathing, Step 2 will deal with techniques of "breathing to sing," as contrasted with your normal "breathing to live." To prepare you to use those techniques to best advantage, Step 1 explores the preliminary attitudes, concepts, and information you will need as you start to apply them to your singing.

CONTENTS OF STEP 1

LESSON 1

A Preliminary Briefing for the Singer

CONCEPTS

So you want to sing?

Fine. This class is a logical starting place, since the subject matter here is your singing voice—and how to improve it.

Let us begin with some basic principles of how your voice works and how to control it. If, as the class proceeds, progress doesn't come to you as quickly as you had hoped, it may be because you haven't given enough consideration to one or more of these principles. Remember, they are *basic*. They underlie all the singing you will do, so it is wise to review them from time to time.

Six Basic Principles of Voice Training

1. *Singing is a do-it-yourself activity.* It's *your* voice. You alone control the thoughts, muscles, and physical coordination that make singing possible for you. Your instructor will give you valuable information and suggestions about singing, but only you can make them work in your voice. Progress cannot be applied from outside. Only *your* concentration, hard work, and persistence can make your voice function in the way you want it to.

2. *You have to want to sing.* The only component of singing that no one else can help you develop very much is your *desire* to sing. Without a strong personal motivation you will make little progress and will become easily discouraged or frustrated. Your friends may have flattered you about what a great voice you have when you sing at parties, but flattery can't overcome the present vocal problems you experience. Your own motivation must be strong enough to keep you going until you master those problems. It must provide the desire that will lead you to do what must be done to make needed changes actually happen.

3. *Instruction is valuable; use it.* Although singing is a do-it-yourself activity, you will soon discover that you do not hear yourself in the way others do when you sing. Since you are usually singing *for* those others, and trying to communicate to them what you want your singing to mean, the difference is crucial. Helpful advice from qualified others can help you shape your singing into the accurate, expressive communication you want it to be. In this realm your instructor is

the expert-in-residence, ready to give you guidance worth following. This book supplies techniques, suggestions, and activities for you to try. Other class members will give their reactions to your singing. These may be among the most helpful comments you will get, since those classmates face singing problems similar to yours.

Your success will depend on how well you *use* the good advice you are given. Unless you put into practice in your voice the constructive suggestions you receive, your singing will not change very much. Your present habits are strong and will continue to control how you sing until they are replaced by more constructive habits.

4. *Develop your curiosity about singing*. Listen. Compare. Experiment. Ask questions. Remember. In order to find out what your voice will do, you must clarify your ideas about what singing requires. This is done best by experiencing for yourself many different kinds and styles of singing. Closely watch and listen to singers performing styles you don't ordinarily listen to, as well as familiar ones. For example, art songs, concert arias, operas, oratorios, and many sacred solos require that the voice be used as a controlled, artistic musical instrument. Try to hear live performances of as many of those styles as you can. Watch famous singers on television. Ask your instructor to recommend current singing "greats" and recordings. Compare what you hear and see with the way you are singing at present. Ask yourself such questions as: What are the differences? Could I sing the way they do? What techniques would I have to learn? What would I have to change? This kind of curiosity about your singing is essential if the instruction given in this class is to be effective in developing your voice. To help stimulate such curiosity, most of the lessons of this book include an On Your Own section, which provides exploratory activities you can do by yourself. Use it.

5. *Make haste slowly*. Control your natural impatience when progress doesn't come as quickly as you wish. Improving your singing involves changes in your habits, your ways of thinking, and many of your insights. Such changes can rarely be rushed. Your singing reflects your individuality, which took years to develop into its present form. You are not going to change that personal identity overnight, so be patient. Persistent application of the techniques and principles given here *can* bring you gradual and steady progress; if you don't let impatience defeat you, it probably *will*.

6. *Singing should feel good*. One of the fundamental joys of resonant, full-toned singing is the way it combines rewarding physical sensation with deep emotional stimulation. It is exhilarating, as you will discover when you are able to sing a favorite song with a rich tone that pleases you. This pleasure in the physical act of making fine singing tone is more basic than "styling" or "expressive singing," important as those become later on. It is a satisfaction that is also available in many exercises. The ability to produce a clear, resonant, accurate tone—*every time you try*—can be a highly rewarding achievement, and that is what many exercises aim to develop. If such a feeling of accomplishment is never present, something is not working right, and you should find out why. Every step toward the kind of singing you want to do should be a stimulating experience rather than a drawn-out technical drudgery.

Good luck!

CLASS ACTIVITIES

1. The class will sing *America* (p. 255) in unison several times, using more than one key. As you sing, consciously use the best tone you can produce, projecting it with confidence. Think about and answer the following questions:

a. What did you actually do to produce the tone you considered your "best"? What would you change to sing some other kind of tone?

b. How do the voices around you sound in comparison with yours? If you were to imitate one of them, what would you have to change?

c. What vocal problems did you have? Were any notes too high or low? What did you do when you came to those notes? Did you strain? Did you run out of breath? Be as specific as you can.

2. The class will be divided into groups of four or five, and each group will sing *America* in front of the class. While others are singing, observe:

   a. What specific things do individuals do that affect how they look and sound? Is their posture good or bad? Do they sing with their mouths closed? Can you hear individuals easily, or do some sing timidly? Do you hear particularly pleasing or harsh sounds from individuals?

   b. What signs of nervousness do you see? Fidgeting or nervous hands? Looking at the floor or ceiling? Excessive "hamming it up"?

   The class will compare individual performances and hold a class critique after all the groups have performed.

3. If time permits, individuals may volunteer to sing by themselves. The class will hold a critique about signs of strong motivation, obvious enjoyment of performing, tone qualities, and so on.

ON YOUR OWN

1. Sing *America* in front of a large mirror. Watch yourself with the same close attention you gave others. Give yourself a similar critique based on the questions used in the Class Activities.

2. Sing a familiar song in another style, consciously trying to be "expressive" in your performance. Watch what you do. In what specific ways is it different from your singing of *America*?

3. Record your performance of *America*, singing with all the care you used for previous performances. On the playback, concentrate on the sound of your singing tone. Is it what you expected? If you wish that it sounded some other way, try to describe how you would like it to be.

LESSON 2

Why Are You Self-Conscious?

CONCEPTS

You say you're a little nervous about singing for all these people? Well, welcome to the group.

Feeling nervous in such a situation is quite natural, but you can overcome it. Some causes of this nervousness apply to everyone, such as being timid in front of strangers, having limited experience in singing, and feeling physical tension. In addition, you may have personal reasons growing out of your experience and unique development. Whatever the causes are, however, you need to confront them squarely. When you do, they will probably turn out to be rather puny giants whose strength comes from banding together back in the shadows of your mind, among your unreasoned fears. Bringing them into the light of conscious thought immediately weakens their power to frighten you.

Four Common Causes of Self-Conscious Nervousness

1. *Uncertainty about what you are going to do.* Since your vocal control is not yet completely dependable, you feel unsure about what will happen when you sing with others listening. This makes you uneasy or tense.

2. *Subconscious fears.* Everyone has normal fears of failing, appearing ridiculous, being laughed at, or being made fun of. Your conscious mind may tell you that such things probably *won't* happen when you sing, but your subconscious mind and your emotions keep whispering to you that they *might*. This undermines your confidence.

3. *Physical tensions.* You may have found that you freeze up, your knees knock, your mouth gets dry, or you feel weak because your pulse is pounding so hard. These are common physical manifestations of your subconscious fears, and you can control them. You may think now that you can't, but you can learn to. When you do, the physical energy they took can be used to help your performance.

4. *Self-consciousness itself.* That's not double-talk. If all you can think about as you start to sing is how nervous you are, that's what you will continue to concentrate on. Nervousness feeds on itself. In a real sense you decide that you will be nervous just by thinking about it, so you *are*.

By simply identifying the major causes of your self-consciousness you can ease much of their subconscious emotional pressure. If you know specifically what troubles you, you can deal with it directly and develop techniques that gradually will cancel out its effects. Try the following techniques.

Four Workable Control Techniques

1. *For uncertainty:* Prepare, plan, study, and practice. Work hard at preparing what you will sing for class. When you find that you can do something better because you are well prepared, your confidence grows. *Replace habits of uncertainty based on inexperience with habits of confidence based on experience.*

2. *For subconscious fears:* Try to name what you are afraid of. Do you fear that the listeners are going to laugh at you? Well, in this class their turns are coming, so they know you could laugh at them; are they likely to laugh at you? Are you afraid you won't get through the song and thus "fail"? It probably won't happen; but, even if it did, how great a tragedy would that be? You can try again and learn from the whole experience. *Use conscious reason to defeat subconscious panic.*

3. *For physical tensions:* Do specific physical things to counteract them. Stand tall, breathe deeply, bend your knees slightly to avoid rigidity, raise your chest, keep your shoulders back and down. Smile at the audience. Draw together a feeling of physical poise before you start to sing by the conscious use of such physical acts. *Don't let physical tensions start.*

4. *For self-consciousness itself:* Think about what you are going to *do*, not about how you *feel*. Concentrate on your posture and breathing. Think of the meaning of the words and the mood you want to convey. There is plenty to think about in the music itself, and the more you focus on such thoughts the less you will think about how nervous you are.

You should accept the fact that performance requires nervous energy, and this usually involves some feeling of tension. Your natural wish to sing well may intensify those feelings. In fact, self-consciousness can be viewed as the conscious awareness of those things you are able to do in performance. Right now you may think of it as fear of what you are unable to do. Nervous tension may be an ingredient of both situations, but in the first case it helps you and in the second it gets in your way. Increased performance experience will bring a growing control of the difference.

CLASS ACTIVITIES

1. Each person will give a brief impromptu talk to the class. Tell your name and such things as what singing you've done, what you hope to learn in this class, what you feel most self-conscious about, and what your opinion is about some current local or national issue. After each person speaks, hold a class discussion about:

    a. What specific actions showed the speaker's nervousness? Common signs include shuffling feet, agitated or awkward hands, saying "uh" or "y'know" frequently, speaking too softly, and looking at the floor or ceiling. Can you discover others?

    b. How did the speaker try to control nervousness? Identify specific actions if you can. If you see something that works well, can you use it when you talk?

2. The class will sing a folksong or round (see pp. 255–91), or Exercise 2.1, together several times. As you sing, observe in detail what you are doing and feeling. Are you nervous or tense when you know others are singing with you? Can you consciously use your "best" voice? Is the song easier to sing when it is repeated, because you are more sure of notes and words?

3. The class will repeat the song or exercise in progressively smaller groups until finally individuals sing by themselves for the class. When you sing alone, compare the feelings you observed in Activity 2 with those experienced in singing by yourself. Which of the causes discussed in the

Concepts section made you self-conscious? Were you able to use any of the remedies given? How much of your nervousness do you feel was simply the result of expecting to be nervous?

Exercise 2.1.   Sing the vowels with an open, relaxed feeling.

ON YOUR OWN

1.   Begin to learn a song designated by the instructor. For guidance, consult Seven Steps to Learning a New Song, Appendix 1, p. 145.

2.   Explain to someone not in this class what he or she might do to overcome self-consciousness when speaking or performing for others. Can you make your ideas clear?

3.   Watch singers on television. Try to determine why they do not appear to be nervous. Be specific—what do they do with posture, hands, voices, eyes, breathing, facial expressions, and so on?

4.   Sing *America* again before your mirror. Why are you not as nervous as when you sang for the class? What do you feel and do that is different?

LESSON 3

How to Build Confidence

CONCEPTS

Just before you jump into a swimming pool you gather confidence, take a deep breath, and balance yourself on your toes. You know the water is deep and wet, and if you're not prepared you could be in trouble. To sing well for an audience you need to make similar preparations, since you know that there are people watching you, and unless you are well prepared your performance could drown in a sea of self-conscious confusion.

What you must have is *poise*, which the dictionary defines as "a stably balanced state; equilibrium; easy, self-possessed assurance of manner; a particular way of carrying oneself with dignity." Some of those terms describe things you can *choose* to do, and a poised state of mind grows out of the successful doing. Confidence in singing results from having made poise your consciously chosen physical condition and state of mind.

Here are some effective, proven techniques that you can do by choice, each of which builds confidence in performance because it makes you act in a poised manner.

Five Proven Poise Builders

1.   *Stand tall*. Don't slouch or try to hide. Posture is examined in detail in Lesson 7, but you should start paying attention to it now, as the first step toward poise. The edge-of-the-pool body position is not a bad beginning model for singing posture. It is clearly a consciously chosen "way of carrying oneself" that puts the body in a vital position and induces deep breathing.

2.   *Breathe deeply*. Remember that the physical act of singing starts with breathing. If you are physically tense, breathing suffers first, so you should make your breathing reduce tension at the outset. An effective way to ease tension is to inhale to your fullest capacity, hold the air in briefly, and then let it out slowly, relaxing all the muscles involved as you do so. Consciously making yourself do this right before you sing is a proven method for gaining a poised feeling. Try it.

3.   *Pretend that you are completely confident*. Be an actor. Pretend that you *are* poised, and then act that way. Put your personal fears and tensions aside just as an actor would. You will discover that simply being able to accomplish confident actions, even by pretending, starts to build your confidence that you can do the things you had nervous doubts about.

4.   *Look 'em in the eye!* The more nervous you feel about having others watch you sing, the more crucial it is that you sing directly *to* them. Don't sing to the floor, the back door, or some spot

out in space. Sing to the people. As long as you avoid looking at the audience, you are evading the real problem, which is your subconscious fear of vague threats you imagine coming from those eyes looking at you. Until you confront that fear squarely, the problem will probably go on defeating you. This is not an easy challenge to overcome, but don't give up too quickly. Use the actor's method of pretending to be what you want to be; you may then find that it is indeed possible for you.

5. *Keep going.* Once you have jumped into the water it is too late to reconsider. You must go ahead and do what must be done. Think of singing for an audience in the same way: Once you start, there is no backing out. Persistence pays off. As you begin to succeed regularly in what you set out to do, you will discover that singing for an audience is pleasantly challenging and brings rewards while you are doing it. The excitement of communicating with those people, and getting back a pleased reaction, is fun. When you experience this, your poise will take a great leap forward.

CLASS ACTIVITIES

In this class session, each person will sing a complete solo song for the rest of the class. The instructor will specify songs to be used; familiar folksongs work well (see pp. 255–88), and any song that can be performed with assurance is suitable. In Lesson 2 we pointed out that a major step toward overcoming nervousness was to prepare adequately. Learn the song thoroughly. Sing it before your mirror. Record it if you can. If the song you use is not in this book, be sure you have music available for the accompanist, so that the accompaniment will be accurate and will support rather than hinder what you do. In your preparation you may want to try some of these devices:

1.   Pretend that you are the most confident, outgoing person you know of—a friend, a public figure, a television personality. Sing with the confidence you think that person would exhibit. Don't try to imitate his or her style, or give an impression of the person's performance, but simply borrow assurance. Sing to the mirror, and observe what you do as you sing this way. Can you carry that over into your class performance?

2.   Try to imitate the style of a well-known singer. This is not a "takeoff," and you should do it without laughter or slapstick. Don't be too concerned with imitating tone quality, since you can't really make the same sound anyway. The aim is simply to borrow confidence from your mental image of the success of this person's style.

3.   While you are practicing, consciously check what you are doing against the list of Five Proven Poise Builders in the Concepts section. Are you using all of them?

ON YOUR OWN

1.   Try some of the suggestions about poise given in this lesson when you are with your friends, but don't tell them what you are doing. To do this, play the role of a confident, outgoing, life-of-the-party type. Compare your feelings as you do this with those you had while singing for the class. Do you notice similarities or differences? Notice how your friends react to your "performance."

2.   Sing another performance before your mirror. This time, pretend that you are the Great Artist in Person, and ham it up. Throw those ravishing tones out to the huddled masses listening to you. (They love you!) Watch closely in the mirror to discover exactly what you do to simulate such confidence. Notice little things: What do you do with your posture, facial expressions, general animation? What relation do all these factors bear to what was said about poise in the Concepts section? Do you see the relation in your own performance?

LESSON 4

Where Does Your Singing Start?

CONCEPTS

How is your left posterior cricoarytenoid?

Didn't know you had one? Well, your voice wouldn't work very well without it. It is one of the muscles that helps control the vocal folds of your larynx—those little gadgets that vibrate to produce the actual vocal sound. And you've been talking all these years without even being aware it was there!

The point is, you probably don't need to know about it—at least to begin with. You speak because you want to say something, rather than from a desire to flex muscles. You feed a mental concept—what you want to say—into the vocal mechanism, and like a computer it does the work, so long as nothing interferes.

In a similar way, you "sing" because you want to "say" ideas with the sounds of singing. Once again, if you let it, the vocal machinery works automatically. The starter button is that "want" you have, the desire to make meaningful sounds by singing. Call it motivation or concept or whatever you wish; if you don't have it, you don't begin. Once it gets the process going, other important questions become relevant—about how you continue and control the meanings you want your singing to say. Here are some of them.

1. *What is your mental image of singing tone?* What is your idea of singing sound as contrasted with other kinds? What do you want yours to sound like? Do you have one clear idea, or several vague ones? Are they clear enough to allow you to make one consistent quality of sound? Do you know how you really sound to others?

2. *How exact are your concepts of language?* Is your speech lazy, or do you make clear, concise sounds? Do you speak with an accent, or do you know whether you do? How accurate are your vowels and consonants? Do you pronounce words correctly and enunciate them clearly? These areas will be explored in Step 4, but you should start listening to yourself now, for lazy speech tends to produce vague, inaccurate singing.

3. *What do you want your singing to mean?* This question may seem too vague to answer specifically, for words often lack the power to explain subtle meanings exactly, but think about it. How do you now use your speaking voice to convey meanings that words *can't* express fully? How do you say the same word in ways that give it different meanings?

4. *How does your voice express your feelings?* How do you convey emotion? You don't use a monotone to express great anger or make love. What do you *do* with your voice to express such feelings? You use the same voice to sing with; can you carry into your singing the inflections and shadings that will convey those emotions?

5. *Can you pay sustained attention?* Do you feed your vocal apparatus a continuous stream of concepts about what you want your singing to say, or do you take mental coffee breaks, hoping that the mechanism will run automatically without guidance? Does nervousness or confusion interrupt the flow of concepts that will give your singing continuous meaning?

6. *Do you have to strain physically to make singing tone?* You probably do not strain when speaking. Does your concept of "singing" lead you to change this when you start producing singing tone? If this happens, what are you doing to produce that strain? Are you able to *let yourself sing,* or do you feel you must *make yourself sing?*

Finding answers to these questions will confirm that your singing starts from and is controlled by your concepts of what you want it to say and mean, rather than from having trained your muscles to act mechanically. Unless this control-by-concept is the source of what you do in singing, much practicing will be pointless, because it will simply repeat vocal mistakes you make by habit, out of uncertainty about tone and what you want it to mean. *Singing starts from knowing why, what, and how you want to sing.* Once it is started, it must rely on a vocal apparatus—your whole body—that has been trained to function in a manner that lets your concepts produce meaningful singing tones without interference.

CLASS ACTIVITIES

1. On a signal from the instructor, do the following things in order without stopping:

> Stand up quickly
> Turn around twice to your right
> Clap your hands over your head three times
> Bow to the front of the room once
> Sing:

> Sit down

Silly? Maybe not. Which of the following statements describes best what happened?

    a. You activated a number of muscles, working singly and in groups, specifying in your mind what each muscle had to do, so that you could produce a complicated series of actions.

    b. You were given a sequence of things to do; after you understood what they were, you went ahead and did them. You gave no thought to muscles but concentrated on what came next; you let the interaction of muscles take care of itself.

Hold a brief class discussion about how this applies to the act of singing.

2. Using Exercises 4.1 and 4.2 or a song designated by the instructor, the class will sing together, applying some of the following moods (or others) to control the way in which the music is sung:

    a. You are very happy because you have just been given a million dollars tax-free.

    b. You are very sad, at the funeral of a close friend.

    c. You are wildly excited because your team has just won the championship.

d. You are very, very much in love, and you feel wonderful.
e. You are angry because someone has just kicked your dog.
f. You are desolate because your loved one has just left you forever.

Since each mood calls for its own sound, as you sing try to discover what you do to make changes, what physical adjustments are necessary, and what thought processes you go through. An important question is, how do you know what happy, sad, excited, angry, and other moods will sound like? After the class has sung together, individuals will be asked to sing by themselves.

Exercise 4.1.

Ah! ——— What — a day!

Exercise 4.2.

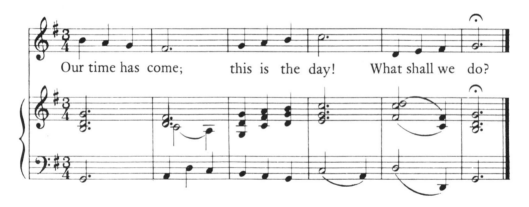

Our time has come;   this is the day!   What shall we do?

ON YOUR OWN

Listen to singers on radio, recordings, and television. Analyze the sounds they make, and try to relate your own singing to those sounds. Try to make some of the sounds, recognizing that you won't really sound like those singers. In order to try to imitate their sounds, however, you have to modify your own concepts of what producing a singing sound involves, so try it. Make a point of listening to styles you are not familiar with. Find the "serious music" radio stations, and listen to programs that include opera, art songs, oratorios, and cantatas. Ask your instructor for guidance in this listening.

LESSON 5

Making Motivation Work for You

CONCEPTS

Why do you want to sing?

We've stressed that your desire to sing is the starter for the singing process. Where does that desire come from? Can you identify your reasons for feeling that singing is something you can do? Such reasons may range from the trivial to the most important. The stronger and more clearly defined they are, the more support they offer in carrying you through the necessarily technical, and sometimes tedious, training process your voice will require.

We are speaking of your *goals* in singing. In short, where do you want to go with it? When you get in your car to drive you have goals, either consciously or subconsciously. You are going somewhere; it may be only to the supermarket, or it may be across the United States. The longer trip requires much greater goal preparation than the shorter, but, in both, certain preliminary conditions must be met. You have to know how to drive; the car must have gas; the motor must run well; you must obey the laws and rules of the road; you cannot expect to abuse your car or ask it to do things it can't do. You start with these basics and then control your activity—driving—in terms of the goal you want it to achieve—getting you to the market or across the country.

The parallel between this and singing should be apparent. There may be someone in this class who will qualify eventually as The Singer—an accomplished professional artist with an established reputation, who makes a fine living by singing. The chances are that most members of the class are instead Others Who Sing—people who use their voices simply for pleasure, expression, creativity, and personal satisfaction. The Singer's goals might be compared to those of the long trip across the country; reaching them will take time, work, and persistent dedication. The Others are on shorter trips and don't expect to go as far with their singing. Yet all need to use the same machines, the same roads, and the same basic rules if they are to reach any goals at all.

How do you determine what your real goals in singing are? While there cannot be one specific answer, comparing your personal motivations with those that have led others into singing may bring you some insights. Here are some questions to ask yourself, to explore what those reasons are:

1. *How realistic are you about what you expect of your singing?* This is an important question whether you are just beginning to sing or have hopes of becoming The Singer. If you are pointing toward

a professional career in *any* style of music, you will need many skills, extensive training, lots of hard work, dogged determination—and probably a good deal of luck—*in addition to a good voice*. Have you considered this adequately? On the other hand, if you say, "That's not for me—I don't have all those things in my plans," you may be selling yourself short. This class, and private voice training, may reveal a potential and an interest you didn't know you had. Examine realistically the various kinds of singing that are open to you before you limit your expectations.

2. *What aspirations attract you to singing?* Here are some categories of inducements that lead people into singing. Your own list may draw on more than one area.

    a. *Commercial achievements*—making a living; getting rich; achieving reputation and fame; becoming a star; making best-selling recordings; gaining influence and power.

    b. *Personal needs*—satisfying an inner urge to be expressive and creative, a personal need to succeed, a desire to be admired, to be the center of attention; pursuing a strong attraction to a particular musical style or personality whom you wish to emulate; fulfilling a conviction that you have a great voice; satisfying a wish to use your voice in connection with another activity such as religious work, teaching, drama, or recreation direction; deriving a personal satisfaction from the act of singing itself.

    c. *Musical rewards*—deriving value from the realm of musical ideas by singing, because music itself "makes sense" to you; enjoying the appeal of established masterpieces in one or more styles for their musical qualities; meeting the intense challenge of being able to reproduce fine music creditably; appreciating the musical values in singing that are completely separate from commercial or personal values in your experience and that bring rewards whether or not those other values are present.

Comparing your own aspirations about singing with this list may lead you to discover some motivations you had not realized you had.

Self-Discipline

Whatever your goals, you will not attain them automatically. Wanting is one thing, achieving is another. A realistic appraisal of your aspirations about singing will make it clear that many obstacles will slow your progress toward success, no matter how committed you are. Persistent vocal problems, slow changes in your habits, the number and complexity of things to be learned, rigorous competition from other singers, a limited number of opportunities for success in the kind of singing you want to do, and other unforeseen problems may all be stumbling blocks.

Yet singing *is* rewarding, and it is very worthwhile to develop the abilities you have, whether they lead you to goals that are near or distant. Progress toward those goals will result from your adding to your training the ingredient that only you can supply: *self-discipline*.

If discipline is thought of as motivation in action rather than some form of restriction or punishment, it becomes a powerful ally in improving your singing. It brings your efforts to train your voice under your control; that is, it "disciplines" them in ways which you manage.

Here are some techniques for making self-discipline work for you. Notice that they are based on your own decision to act.

1. *Learn to concentrate.* Focus your mind on what you are doing, and don't let it wander. Observe exactly what does and does not happen. Then make changes because you want to do something you have observed or thought about, not just changes by accident. Notice whether the changes really take place. Don't let your mind slide into neutral while your voice makes random noises.

2. *Make a plan.* Don't leave your singing to chance. Do something about it every day on a schedule you have drawn up. Use techniques introduced in class to prepare for future class assignments. Keep going according to plan, even when you feel frustrated with your lack of progress. Give singing activities high priority in your personal schedule so that they aren't easily

pushed aside. Don't put things off. Are you, yourself, the easiest person you can talk out of doing what ought to be done?

3. *Do it yourself—you might like it!* Don't wait to be coaxed; only you can make necessary changes in your voice. Try to incorporate valuable suggestions about your singing on your own initiative rather than waiting for someone to force you to do it. Often the technique you need the most will seem the most difficult or new, but don't be put off by the fact. Try it.

4. *Broaden your singing experiences.* To restrict yourself to one musical style too quickly limits your growth. If you are attracted strongly to a particular style now, you may feel that singing for you can be limited to that idiom. If this involves trying to imitate a particular voice or personality, you are on a dead-end street. You cannot really do such an imitation successfully, for what you want to imitate is only one facet of what made that person successful. The success you want must come from within you, no matter how you define success. This is done best by building a broad base of musical experiences. Don't specialize too quickly, even though eventually—if you're taking that long trip—you may want to do so. At this point you need to listen to, study, and sing many styles, with initial emphasis on some you now consider uncongenial. In your first years of singing you should plan to sing selections from art songs, German *lieder,* operas, oratorios, light operas, musical comedies, folksongs, sacred songs, and popular standards, to list the most basic.

Remember, singing requires *self*-discipline. You must realize that no one else really cares as much as you do whether you sing well, so you can't blame others if you don't improve. If you put off learning and preparing for this class, or plan to "fake it" when your turn to sing comes around, what you are really doing is frustrating your own "want to" about singing.

CLASS ACTIVITIES

1. The class will learn one of the following simple folksongs and sing it as a group exercise: *On Top of Old Smoky,* p. 280; *Down in the Valley,* p. 269; *All Through the Night,* p. 256; or *Auld Lang Syne,* p. 258. As you are singing, concentrate on the following questions about what you are doing:

    a.   Are you singing notes and rhythms correctly? Do you know whether or not you are?

    b.   Are you singing accurate vowel colors and clear consonants? Do you know whether or not you are?

    c.   What do you do when you come to hard spots in the melody, such as high notes or long phrases? Do you make bad sounds, strain, or just drop out because you feel you can't do it? Try to notice what others are doing in those places.

2. Add different moods or dramatic situations to the song as you did in Exercises 4.1 and 4.2 (p. 12). Examine exactly what you do to make these changes in mood or meaning.

3. Class members will sing Activities 1 and 2 as solos. As others sing, follow them closely and ask the same questions about what they are doing.

4. The instructor will specify other changes in the way the song is to be sung (such as pretending you are singing for a large audience, in a very intimate situation, or with an exaggerated jaw opening). As you sing, determine whether the changes requested actually happen in your voice, or whether your old habits prevented anything new from happening.

5. As a written assignment, make a work schedule and a set of personal objectives for this course:

    a.   List your personal objectives for your voice in this class. What specific improvements do you hope to make in the way you sing? What changes in tone, breathing, diction, control of nerves, or improved expressive ability are you seeking?

    b.   Specify how much time you intend to devote each week to singing, in hours and minutes.

    c.   List the styles of music you are most interested in singing, with reasons for each choice.

ON YOUR OWN

Over a period of two or three weeks, keep a log of every time you hear any sort of singing performance. List when it happened, what was sung (as nearly as you can identify it), where you heard it (radio, recording, television, live performance), what style of music it was, and about how long it took. Make an effort to hear enough singing to give this project some personal value.

LESSON 6

Your Phonation Machine

CONCEPTS

Phonation means making sound with the voice. You have been phonating all your life in many ways. Some of these have qualified as singing, which is simply a specialized, closely controlled form of phonation.

The mechanism that produces this sound is delicate and complex. To refer to it as your *voice* is a simplification much like calling your car your *wheels* because it's so easy to see them going around as you move. A lot more of you than the small parts making the actual sound is involved. Your whole body takes part in the process, and we will refer to it here as *your phonation machine*. The rest of this book will study in detail how the various parts of the machine participate in making that specialized, controlled sound that you want to produce.

At the outset it is important to realize that the machine must operate as one smoothly working unit. Like the works of a fine watch, it functions best by precision, coordination, and freedom from interference. Singing uses your whole being, not just separately operating mechanisms for thinking, breathing, sound making, and resonating. Most of the muscles that make it work cannot be located by sensation, like that left posterior cricoarytenoid we spoke of, and so many are involved that you couldn't keep track of them individually.

The diagrams on pp. 18–20 represent the most important active parts of your phonation machine. Figure 6.1 locates four principal systems and their component parts. In approximately chronological order of their involvement in the tone-making process, these are:

1. *The Starter.* This is the brain, where concepts of singing are formulated to be delivered to the other systems through the central nervous system. This process was examined in Lesson 4.

2. *The Motor.* The breathing system, which is studied in detail in Step 2, takes the most body space of all the systems in these diagrams. It also relies on the strength and support of the muscles of the legs, hips, shoulders, and entire trunk. The costal muscles and diaphragm make actual breathing happen.

3. *The Vibrator.* This makes the sound. Figures 6.2 and 6.4 enlarge the specific areas and parts, to allow you to see the relationships involved. Lessons 11–14 examine the nature of the tones that are produced by this mechanism.

4. *The Resonator.* This system amplifies, shapes, and projects tone in the exact form heard by listeners. Figure 6.3 shows its major parts. The various functions of the system are studied in Lesson 15 and Step 4.

Figure 6.1. The Systems of the Phonation Machine

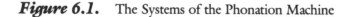

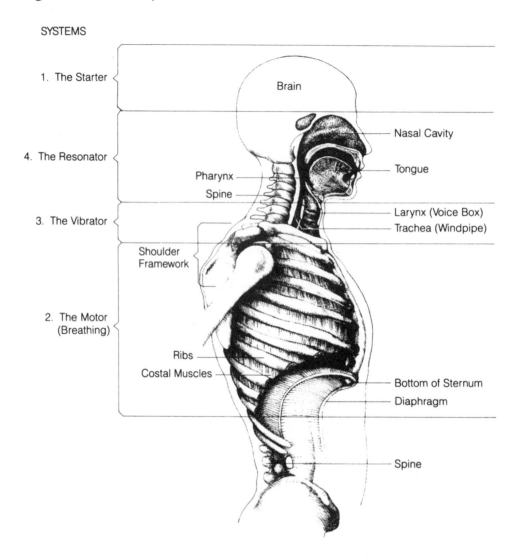

SYSTEMS

1. The Starter

4. The Resonator

3. The Vibrator

2. The Motor
(Breathing)

Brain

Nasal Cavity

Tongue

Pharynx
Spine

Larynx (Voice Box)
Trachea (Windpipe)

Shoulder
Framework

Ribs
Costal Muscles

Bottom of Sternum
Diaphragm

Spine

How the Machine Works

Here is a one-paragraph description of how the phonation machine works:

The brain forms concepts of the singing desired—tone, words, expression. To start the process, it informs the other systems by impulses sent simultaneously through the central nervous system. This causes the breathing muscles to inhale by a process called diaphragmatic-costal breathing. When a controlled amount of air is in position in the lungs, the process is reversed, and a controlled stream of air is sent up through the trachea to the larynx. The arytenoid cartilages in the larynx revolve, bringing the vocal folds into approximation (next to each other), so that they vibrate when the air stream is pushed through them by pressure from below. This produces sound waves. The intensity and pitch of the sound waves are controlled by the combined action of tension placed on the folds by the cartilages and pressure of the air stream. The sound waves go out through the pharynx and mouth, where they are resonated, given vowel shapes, and articulated into word units. Articulation is done by insertion of consonants into the stream of sound through the action of tongue, teeth, and lips.

It is essential to remember that the sequence of events being described is *one continuous, unified action*. The singing it produces is a single product that exists only in time. It cannot be

Figure 6.2. The Larynx, Top View

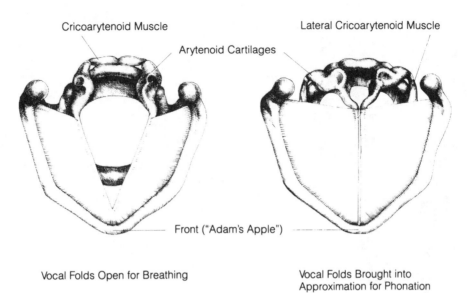

Cricoarytenoid Muscle

Arytenoid Cartilages

Lateral Cricoarytenoid Muscle

Front ("Adam's Apple")

Vocal Folds Open for Breathing

Vocal Folds Brought into
Approximation for Phonation

Figure 6.3. The Vibrator and Resonator Systems

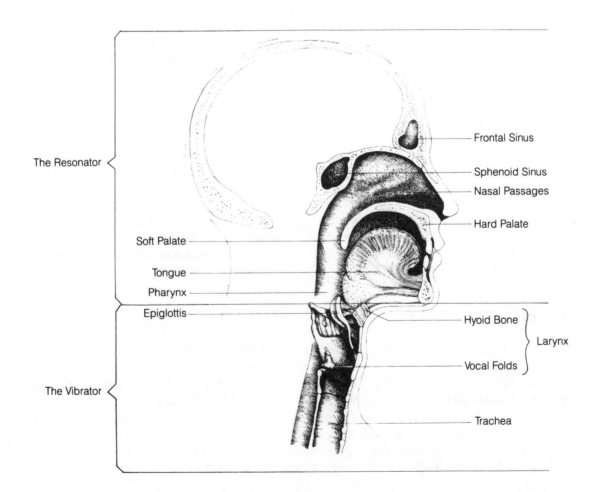

The Resonator

The Vibrator

Soft Palate

Tongue

Pharynx

Epiglottis

Frontal Sinus

Sphenoid Sinus

Nasal Passages

Hard Palate

Hyoid Bone

Larynx

Vocal Folds

Trachea

Figure 6.4. The Larynx, Side View

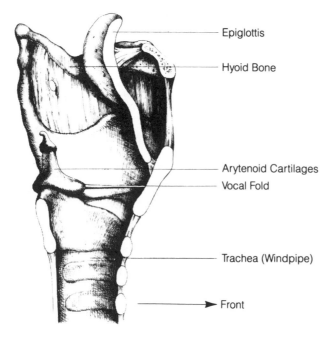

Epiglottis

Hyoid Bone

Arytenoid Cartilages
Vocal Fold

Trachea (Windpipe)

➤ Front

subdivided and still retain its meaning. In the plainest terms, it all happens at once, or it doesn't happen at all.

When you buy a new automobile you expect to get more than just fine tires, a smoothly running motor, good brakes, a dependable electric system, and so on. You want the whole car, a machine that will work for you as a unified mechanism, with smooth coordination, precision, and ease. If one of its major systems doesn't work, the rest won't do much either, so you won't have an effective transportation machine. This is a good analogy for the operation of your phonation machine, and it embodies a view about singing that you should keep in mind as we begin the study of its component parts in Step 2.

It may have struck you that you have been making sounds—phonating—all your life without all this detailed analysis of what you were doing, so why is it necessary now? There are two answers. First, the vocal demands of singing are much more exacting than those of speaking, so that more sensitive controls of the phonation machine are essential. Secondly, you aim to sing *expressively.* You expect that the sounds your machine makes will have specific, subtle, emotional meanings. Such meanings cannot occur until phonation is clear, controlled, and accurate. Fortunately this is the kind of sound making that feels good, so that mastering it is a pleasant process. When it is working for you dependably, expressive singing is your next step.

CLASS ACTIVITIES

1. With the tip of your index finger, locate the small V-shaped notch right above the tip of your Adam's apple. Hold your finger there very lightly and say AH or sing in a low tone. Notice that immediately you feel vibration in the tip of your finger. This is because the fingertip is right at one end of the vocal folds. Extend this exploration through the following steps:

    a.   Sing Exercise 6.1, and see whether the Adam's apple rises as you sing up the scale. If it does, try to sing in a manner that leaves it in the original position. (*Note: Do not try to hold it down! Exert no pressure whatever.*) On which tones do you feel the greatest vibration? It should be the lower tones, which have a longer, slower vibration rate.

b.   Open your jaw as if yawning. Put the index finger of one hand in the depression the yawn creates right in front of your ear, and put the index finger of the other hand on your Adam's apple again. Once more sing Exercise 6.1, several times in succession, until you can perform it with virtually no movement (other than vibration) being felt by either finger. Does the lack of jaw and throat movement give you the feeling that the tone is being produced deeper down in your body?

c.   Remove both fingers from the positions of b, stand in a comfortable tall posture, and sing Exercise 6.1 once more. Can you duplicate the feeling of open, relaxed throat, deep tone production?

Exercise 6.1.

2.   Sing a familiar song for recording and playback. Consciously observe the operation of your phonation machine as you sing; that is, notice the actual quality of each tone. When the quality changes, do you both hear and feel it? Can you identify what makes the change happen? Does it occur because something in the melody is difficult to produce? Does the difficulty have any relation to something your phonation machine does or fails to do?

ON YOUR OWN

1.   Watch singers in live performances, recitals, church services, television appearances, and motion pictures. See as many different styles as possible. Do these performers make singing look easy or as if it were work? Is there a correlation between how they look and how they sound? Does their singing make you aware of the functions of the phonation machine or let you concentrate on the music they are singing?

2.   After watching a successful performance, sing before your mirror, using a familiar song. Can you carry into your performance any of the smooth control of the phonation machine that you observed in the successful singer?

Breathing to Sing

Breathing begins the physical act of singing and continues to support every phase of the process. Controlled breathing makes the phonation machine run. Singers quickly discover that "breathing to sing" is much more demanding than the automatic "breathing to live" they have been doing all their lives. Step 2 examines in detail how the breathing-to-sing process works.

CONTENTS OF STEP 2

LESSON 7

Posture: Let Yourself Sing

CONCEPTS

How well does your car run with one flat tire?

No matter what fine shape the rest of the car is in, that one problem throws everything out of line, and the whole car is prevented from working as it should. It should be apparent that a similar problem would prevent your phonation machine from working the way you want it to. If poor posture lets you fall into an awkward, slouched, or cramped position, you are in effect giving your phonation machine a "flat tire," and as a result your singing will go nowhere.

Remember, *singing is a single, unified act.* It must happen as one smooth, continuous sequence, with all of its component parts working together. For it to begin correctly, the phonation machine must be in a position that allows the sequence to happen without interference. That position is *correct singing posture,* which is based upon two broad principles:

1. *Correct singing posture places the body in a position that makes singing possible.* It is "correct" simply because it prepares your physical mechanism to respond to your mental concepts without interference, and it allows the whole process to continue without interruption. It is not an artificial or rigid position, and it must always be an integral part of singing itself.

2. *Posture for singing must be balanced, poised, and resilient.* Body muscles are neither rigid nor flaccid. Most concepts of tensing and relaxing represent extremes that interfere with correct posture and should be avoided. Productive posture for singing closely resembles that for dancing, diving, or boxing.

A basic habit you must develop for effective singing is to assume correct posture automatically as the first preparatory act. This eliminates many mistakes before they happen, by not allowing a "flat tire" to put the machine in a poor position. Following this, habitual correct posture allows proper breathing to become a habit, and you will discover that *proper breathing is virtually impossible without correct posture.*

Here is a detailed anatomical description of the positions various parts of the body must be in to make up the total correct singing posture.

Correct Singing Posture—Standing

Feet	Slightly apart, one a little in front of the other. The weight of the body is slightly forward on the balls of the feet, not back on the heels.

Knees	Flexibly loose, never rigidly locked.
Hips	Rolled slightly forward in line with the body. Firm up those "bustle muscles," and do not let the buttocks protrude to the rear unnaturally.
Abdomen	Flat, firm, held in comfortably, but not rigid.
Chest	Held high, but not in a strained or artificial position. It must not collapse or move up and down when you breathe; it remains essentially motionless.
Shoulders	Held back and down. They must not hunch up during breathing.
Arms	Dropped at the sides in a natural position. Forget them if you can. If you are holding music, hold it comfortably so that you can see it without bending your head, but don't hold your arms so high that they look like wings.
Hands	Relaxed and unobtrusive; forget them if possible. Don't let them fidget, creep into pockets, go behind your back, or assume unnatural positions. Above all, keep them still.
Head	Chin about parallel to the floor, never pointing out and up. Imagine that you are suspended from the ceiling by a hook in the back part of your head, on a line your spine would follow if it extended up through your skull. See Figure 7.1.

Figure 7.1. Correct Standing Singing Posture

Correct Singing Posture—Seated

From the hips up	Essentially the same as correct standing posture.
Feet	Both feet flat on the floor; do not cross them, or hold them at strained angles.
Legs	Placed in a position that gives balance and firm support to the entire body.
Back	Held *away* from a chair or other support; in effect, lean on your own spine—not anything else. See Figure 7.2.

Figure 7.2. Correct Seated Singing Posture

CLASS ACTIVITIES

1. Place your heels against a flat wall. Try to make your calves, buttocks, shoulders, and head touch the wall, even though the position may feel awkward. Relax as much tension out of it as you can, and then go through the following steps:

    a.   Without moving your feet, shift the weight of your body forward until you almost stand on your toes; maintain the rest of your position. Try to establish the feeling of buoyancy you would have before diving into a swimming pool.

    b.   Step away from the wall a few inches and resume the buoyant position. Put one hand on your upper chest below the collarbones. Inhale deeply, hold the air to a count of five, and then exhale with a prolonged, loud hiss. Does your chest move up and down with your breathing? Repeat this until you can do it with no chest motion, keeping the chest in a high position that will allow your breathing to be deep.

    c.   Put one hand on your upper abdomen, right below where your ribs join in front. Breathe in and out, deeply. Try to feel expansion right under your hand, as though you were putting the air right there. Repeat several times, consciously relaxing your throat muscles.

2. Sit down and relax completely; then stand again, taking the correct singing posture outlined

above. Check each item from the ground up. Compare this posture with the one you assumed at the wall and then with what you consider your normal posture. Are there differences you can identify in each case?

3.   The class will sing Exercise 7.1 or a song designated by the instructor. Concentrate on assuming correct singing posture before you begin, and try not to change it as you are singing. Can you sing the whole piece without changing?

4.   Individuals will sing the exercise or songs for class critiques. While others are singing, concentrate on their posture control. Does their posture seem natural or strained? Are they able to maintain it all the way through their singing? Can you suggest ways in which they might improve it?

Exercise 7.1.

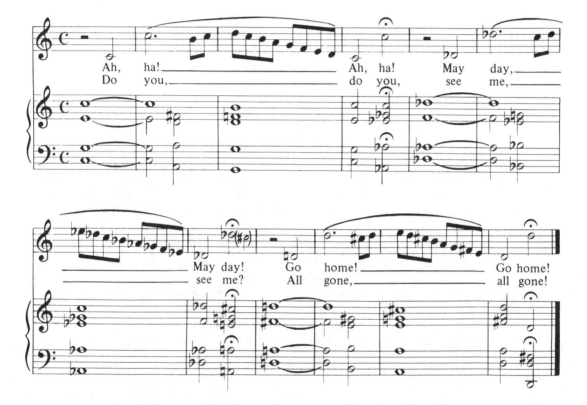

ON YOUR OWN

1.   Go to your mirror in light clothing. Watching yourself closely, experiment with posture in the following ways:

   a.   Stand in what you feel is your normal, comfortable, easy posture.

   b.   Take the posture outlined in the Concepts section. What changed?

   c.   Slouch into what you know is a bad posture. What changed this time? Note your physical sensations in all three postures.

   d.   Stand on your toes, raising both arms in front of you as though preparing to dive. Observe the movements of your shoulders, chest, abdomen, and hips. Did you also take a breath without thinking about it? Why?

2.   Watching yourself in the mirror, hold this book in a singing position. Do your arms seem natural and easy or rigidly held? Lower the book to your side, then raise it again. What moves in your body as you bring it up? Can you do this without distorting your entire posture?

LESSON 8

Breathing to Sing

CONCEPTS

Have you ever observed how a baby breathes when it is sleeping?

You can see clearly how the natural breathing system works, expanding and contracting gently just above the center of the infant's body. The baby has not had lessons in breathing and really knows nothing about it; it breathes instinctively to stay alive. The system does all the mechanical work of breathing, supplying needed air without any conscious control on the baby's part. This is the beginning of the breathing to live that we all do, and it is the principal foundation on which breathing to sing is built. Both types use the same apparatus, operate in much the same way, and are controlled by habit, but breathing to sing is far more demanding and coordinated. Simply defined, this is breathing that *makes singing possible*.

Once habits of correct posture are working for you, the next step is to learn further techniques for breathing to sing. It has to become your automatic way of breathing in response to your desire to sing, and it must eventually be controlled by habit. As long as you must consciously remind yourself to breathe that way, you will never sing very well; you will be too busy thinking about breathing.

Breathing to sing has two principal purposes:

1. To support your production of continuous, controlled singing tone.
2. To make it possible to sing meaningful phrases and expressive nuances.

In order to fulfill these objectives, your breathing system must work in a more sophisticated, coordinated way than when you are only breathing to live. When you speak, you rarely sustain single sounds very long. By contrast, singing is a succession of sustained tones on pitch. This characteristic of singing requires a continuous flow of air pressure for phonation, and you have to adjust your breathing system to provide it. Adding phrasing and expression to singing intensifies even more the need for a controlled air flow. You not only are making continuous tone but also must have the support to add the tonal shapes, colors, and dynamic shadings that make singing expressive.

Proper breathing to sing is the most complete use of the technique called *diaphragmatic-costal breathing*. The term is derived from the names of the muscles involved, which may help you remember it. *Diaphragmatic* refers to the function of the diaphragm, the large muscle lying across the body under the lungs. Its up-and-down motion supplies the impetus to the bottom of the breathing system. *Costal* refers to the muscles of the sides, ribs, and lower back, which form a web that works together with the diaphragm to control intake and outflow of air in the lungs. Study Figure 8.1 carefully. Four principles help explain how this technique works.

Four Principles of Diaphragmatic-Costal Breathing

1. *Diaphragmatic-costal breathing makes room for the air.* Air is under pressure all around you; if you make room for it in your lungs, that pressure will push it in. You cannot *take* a breath in the sense of reaching out for it; you have no muscles to do that kind of reaching. Instead, the action of the diaphragm and the costal muscles creates room that allows the air to come in. Understanding this principle and how it works in your own breathing may help you not to work so hard.

2. *Your ribs form a cage that shelters diaphragmatic-costal breathing.* Most of the muscles involved in this kind of breathing are inside or under the ribs and will work properly only if they are allowed room and freedom. The rib cage must never be allowed to drop down on them or restrict their action. The chest position detailed in Lesson 7 is essential because of this principle, and it should be strictly observed.

3. *The chief function of the throat in breathing is to get out of the way.* It must not tighten, as though trying to grab a breath. Wind blowing through a crack will whistle, and very little gets through; but coming through a wide-open door it makes no sound even though a great deal gets through. If you can hear yourself breathe while you sing, you know you are getting in your own way and working far too hard for too little return. Develop a habit of opening your throat to an out-of-the-way position that allows air to pass easily.

Figure 8.1. Diaphragmatic-Costal Breathing

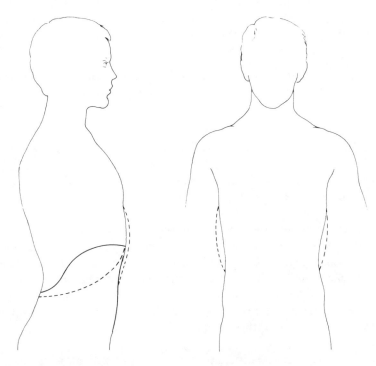

Correct Diaphragmatic Breathing   Correct Costal Breathing

Dotted Lines: Inhalation
Solid Lines: Exhalation

4. *Diaphragmatic-costal breathing has a low center of gravity.* Most of the principal muscles involved are low in the trunk of the body, well under the shoulders and throat. You should think of your breathing as happening right below where your ribs join in front. That is where the room is and where the air must go for maximum control. Trying to breathe in the upper chest or under the shoulders simply works against the way your body is built.

Diaphragmatic-costal breathing is the most natural kind because it allows the body to work in the way it is constructed to do. Any other kind you may hear of, such as "high-chest" or "shallow" breathing, is of little use in singing and may actually interfere with it. If bad habits have caused your diaphragmatic-costal breathing to get lazy, it is essential to restore full operation of the system as the basis of successful singing.

Hazards to the Breathing System

Breathing, and the welfare of the system that accomplishes it, is so essential to successful singing that the conscientious singer must be aware of and vigorously guard against conditions and actions that can impede or damage the system. In normal living we are so accustomed to not thinking about breathing that recognizing these hazards should be viewed as a new and essential consideration, perhaps one more of the exacting demands placed upon the singer by the need for breathing to sing. Hazards that threaten vocal production are:

1. *Colds and allergies.* People especially subject to such problems should get the most expert medical help available, as soon as possible, and continue a health program that will do everything possible to control the difficulty. The professional singer learns the importance of this very early and works hard at maintaining control.

2. *Smoking.* Don't smoke. A singer who does so makes a foolish—even stupid—mistake. Tobacco smoke not only irritates the entire breathing system and can lead to cancer but also can cause irreparable damage to the membranes of the throat and nasal passages. Smoking simply risks the destruction of the very mechanism that allows singing to happen.

3. *Chemical irritants.* Swimming in treated pools or salt water invites irritation of throat and nose by the chemical substances in the water; it can easily make singing impossible for several hours. This irritation tends to congest the breathing system, because the body excretes excess amounts of phlegm to counteract it.

4. *Poor health.* Lack of physical activity leads to weakened muscles and poor general body tone. This diminishes the body's ability to react fully to the demands of breathing, leading to shortness of breath and other problems. Singing is a *vital* activity, which means (according to the dictionary) that it "exists as a manifestation of life." It cannot be done by a sluggish body.

While these warnings may seem too obvious to need mentioning, they are easily overlooked. Just as you would not drive your car with a flat tire or one spark plug missing, even though you could make the car move (with resulting damage to tires or engine), so it is simply foolish to try to operate your phonation machine under the strain of potentially damaging hazards that could be prevented.

Habitual diaphragmatic-costal breathing has many tangible personal benefits, for both your singing and your individual well-being. Among these are:

1. Your total breath capacity increases. The technical term for this is *vital capacity*, which points up again that breathing is indeed a "manifestation of life."

2. Breathing—your personal control of air intake and outflow—becomes physically easier, more accurate, and pleasantly invigorating.

3. Your feelings of physical poise and self-confidence increase.

4. Your throat becomes increasingly free from tension while you sing.

5. You are able to concentrate on tone quality, meaning, and expression as you sing, because you don't have to think about the mechanics of breathing.

6. Your general physical health will probably improve.

CLASS ACTIVITIES

1. The class will stand in a large circle so that each person can see the others as they perform the activity. Do the following:

    a. Stand in the correct singing posture outlined in Lesson 7.

    b. Practice inhaling and exhaling in the manner described in this lesson. Don't let your chest rise and fall; try to feel expansion right under the joining of the ribs.

    c. Inhale to the fullest capacity, and, on a signal from the instructor, exhale in a loud hiss for as long as you can, while the instructor counts slowly. Try to feel the pressure of the hiss at the tongue and the diaphragm, *not* in the throat. Notice at which count you run out of breath. When the exercise is repeated, try to extend the hiss two counts further. What do you do to make this happen? Take in more air? Control the outflow better? Where do you feel the control happening? Did your chest collapse when you ran out of air?

2. Sing Exercise 8.1, using the same counting technique. Use several keys in succession, to discover whether one part of your range is easier to use than another. Sing a loud, full, clear tone that does not change the AH vowel. Can you sing the same tone quality right up to where you run out of breath? Does it get weak or breathy? Do you feel strain in your throat as you run out of breath? If so, you are using muscles that should remain open and easy. Can you sing the entire exercise without letting your chest fall or collapse?

3. Using *All Through the Night* (p. 256), or another song chosen by the instructor, sing the song keeping each phrase intact—that is, on one breath that does not weaken or run out before the end of the phrase. Inhale only where there is a rest in the music or a breathing mark (ʼ). Consciously breathe in the diaphragmatic-costal manner described in this lesson. Try to watch others as you sing, to notice what their breathing looks like, whether it is done correctly or incorrectly. Compare what you are doing with what you see.

Exercise 8.1. Transpose to keys between E♭ (low) and C (high).

ON YOUR OWN

1.   Starting with the On Your Own activities given in Lesson 7 (p. 27), add deep breathing as outlined in this lesson. In your mirror watch closely to see what moves and what remains still as you breathe in the diaphragmatic-costal manner. Associate your physical feelings with what you see. Does the deepest breath, which expands you above the waistline, have a different feeling from a breath in which no expansion is visible?

2.   Sing a familiar song before your mirror, trying to make complete phrases as you did in the Class Activities. When you run out of breath at the end of a phrase, do you take time to breathe correctly, or do you try to grab the air? What differences can you see between the two techniques?

LESSON 9

Breath Control: Diaphragmatic-Costal Breathing in Action

CONCEPTS

When you blow up a balloon, you can easily control the air inside—just pinch the neck.

For singing, that kind of control is exactly *wrong,* yet some singers seem to have trouble avoiding it. You may have seen someone whose face gets red when he or she sings and whose tone sounds as though the person were wearing a tight necktie. The problem is sometimes flippantly called "necktie tenor" even though it can trouble both men's and women's voices. Such singers seem, indeed, to be "pinching the neck."

There can be no doubt that air taken into the lungs for singing must be controlled if it is to serve the purpose of producing delicate vibrations of the vocal folds. Because of this, the term *breath control* is often used to denote one of the basics of singing that it is assumed everyone understands. Exactly what is breath control? Does it differ from normal breathing? What relation does it bear to *breath support*—another term used in singing? How do you develop the breath control you need for your singing? Here are some general principles about the term that may help clear up uncertainties you may have:

1. *Breath control means using diaphragmatic-costal techniques for the complete cycle of breathing— inhaling and exhaling.* Since breathing happens in the area below the front of the rib cage, it is easy to understand that the muscles there control inhaling. It may be harder to see that the same muscles must also control exhaling, particularly if you have come to feel such control somewhere in your throat, as sometimes happens. If it were possible when blowing up a balloon to hold on to the sides and bottom, there would be no need to pinch the neck. You could control the air inside by the pressure of your hands. In effect, that is the kind of control needed for singing. The muscles at the bottom and sides of the breathing system—the diaphragmatic-costal muscles—do what your hands would do on the balloon, controlling both the intake and outflow of air. Trying to control breathing at the throat, by straining muscles, arching the tongue, or restricting it in any way, is simply pinching the neck and is *always* damaging to singing.

If you run out of breath when singing a phrase, your first reaction may be, "I need to take in more air." What is probably needed instead is to let less out. This requires better control of exhalation, to let out only enough air, at the right pressure, to make the vocal folds vibrate at the desired rate, without wasting any. That statement is also a very accurate description of breath support, since it explains how tone production receives air support from underneath. This makes it clear that the terms *breath control* and *breath support* are really different explanations of the same process.

2. *Breath control must become your automatic response to the impulse to sing.* You rarely run out of breath when you talk. Why? Not because you are thinking about "breath control"; you want your speaking to convey meaning, and you don't think about breathing at all. Your system responds automatically by getting and controlling enough air to say what you want to say. Breathing to sing—which is really breath control—works in the same way, as was discussed in Lesson 8. Your system automatically adjusts to the additional demands of singing by supplying the air pressure that allows you to make sustained tone and then shape it expressively. The habitual, "not-thinking-about-it" nature of the process is the essential element in providing the effective support you need for sustained singing.

3. *Your personal breath control can be only as effective as you make it.* As far as you are concerned, the crucial question about breathing soon becomes, "All of this theory is fine, but does it work in *my* voice?" Breathing-to-sing breath control is only one form of diaphragmatic-costal breathing used by the body; in order for it to supply maximum benefit to your singing, you must experience its physical sensations for yourself. When you run up a flight of stairs, jog for a mile, or swim the length of the pool under water, your system breathes in diaphragmatic-costal ways, in each case accommodating to the needs of the activity. None of these ways would be quite right for singing, which requires specific adjustments and controls. It is these requirements that you must personally and physically experience in order to make breathing to sing the habit it must become. As you build toward this habit, you need to observe carefully and in detail what you *do* in breathing, to eliminate undesirable activities and accumulate productive experiences that demonstrate that the theory *does* work in your voice.

Here is a checklist of the kinds of questions you should ask yourself in building desirable breathing habits:

1. Do your shoulders move, or hunch forward, as you breathe? (They shouldn't.)

2. Does your chest rise and fall as you breathe? (It should stay quite still.)

3. Does your throat grab for air or gasp to get breath? (It should stay open and relaxed.)

4. Do the muscles and cords of your neck tense up and stand out as you breathe and sing? (You are working too hard and in the wrong way.)

5. Can you hear yourself breathe? (Your throat is closed.)

6. Is your jaw rigidly closed or tense as you breathe? (You are putting a barrier in the way of breathing.)

7. Do you feel your breathing in your throat? (You are probably pinching the neck; go lower!)

8. Does the roof of your mouth dry out as you breathe? (You are probably arching your tongue or closing your throat.)

9. Have you discovered what the low center of gravity in breathing (p. 30) actually *feels* like? (Feels good, doesn't it?)

10. Do you get red in the face when you sing? (You are pinching the neck!)

11. Does your singing tone sound breathy, as though air were escaping around it? (You are wasting breath; see Lesson 25.)

12. When you inhale deeply, what expands? (Compare what you do with the diagrams on p. 29.)

13. Is your vital capacity (total breath capacity) increasing because you are paying more attention to proper breathing techniques? (Review Exercise 8.1, p. 31.)

14. Is correct singing posture habitual with you, or do you slump? (Review Lesson 7.)

CLASS ACTIVITIES

1. The class will sing Exercise 9.1 together as a group and then individually for class critiques. Notice that each phrase is longer than the preceding one and that breathing marks (,) are placed between phrases. Breathe deeply at every breathing mark, and sing each phrase in one breath. The final phrase contains 24 counts, and the challenge is to sustain your tone to the end without weakening it or trying to rush the tempo. In the critique of individual performances, comment on specific problems observed, such as poor posture, audible breathing, heaving chest or shoulders, and breathy tone. (*Note:* Some singers may experience brief dizziness as a result of extended deep breathing. This effect is called *hyperventilation* and is caused by increasing the discharge rate of carbon dioxide from the blood with deep breathing. It is nothing to worry about in normal circumstances; the singer should just sit down and relax, and it will pass.)

2. The class will sing *Believe Me, If All Those Endearing Young Charms* (p. 260) as a group and then individually. Notice that the words are actually one continuous sentence and that the phrases are especially long. To use this as a breathing exercise, do the following:

   a. Sing as far into the song as you can on one breath, marking exactly where you ran out.

   b. Sing it a second time, extending your phrase by as many notes as you can.

   c. Read aloud the words of the first two lines in a way that makes clear that they are really one long, continuous phrase: "Believe me, if all those endearing young charms, which I gaze on so fondly today, were to fade by tomorrow and fleet in my arms like fairy gifts fading away. . . ." Can you read the entire passage in one breath, with meaning? Why can you do it in speaking and not in singing? Study the meaning of the words; what are you *saying*?

   d. Try to sing the first two lines on one breath, while at the same time conveying the meaning you were able to speak.

3. Under the close supervision of the instructor, members of the class will shout "Hah!" or "Hey!" as though trying to attract someone's attention across a football field. Observe the way you breathe when you do this. Shout first so that you feel intense resistance and closing in your throat, and then a second time so that you feel almost nothing in your throat because the tone is so much deeper and more resonant. Which of the two makes you breathe more deeply? Which one uses more of the diaphragmatic-costal breathing mentioned earlier? Which tone would carry further? Which is a better model for singing?

Exercise 9.1.

ON YOUR OWN

1. Lie flat on the floor or on some other hard surface and put a book or two on your upper abdomen. Place one hand on the upper chest and breathe deeply in and out. What moves? Do the books go up and down? Does your hand move? Does your throat feel tense or relaxed? (If diaphragmatic-costal breathing is happening, the books will rise and fall gently, your hand will feel little or no motion, and your throat will feel at ease. You might think of putting the air right under the books.)

2. Stand in a correct singing posture and try to duplicate the feelings in chest, abdomen, and throat that you obtained lying down.

3. Using your mirror, repeat Class Activity 1. When you start to run out of breath, observe what signs of muscular tension appear in your face, throat, upper chest, and abdomen. Can you run out of breath with absolutely no strain or tension becoming apparent in your face and throat? What would you say this has to do with your breath control or breath support?

LESSON 10

Breath Support as the Foundation of Singing

CONCEPTS

A contractor never builds a house from the roof down.

He begins by consulting clear plans, preparing the ground, and building a strong foundation. Only then can he add walls, ceilings, doors, windows, and finally the roof. Unless he starts with a good foundation, anything he tries to build will fall down.

Building a voice is very similar. You can't expect to put on the roof (artistic singing) until you have drawn plans (developed clear concepts of what you want to sing), prepared conditions that will make singing possible (developed assurance, poise, and correct posture), and laid a firm foundation (established habits of diaphragmatic-costal breathing).

The realization that correct breathing is the foundation of virtually everything else involved in the physical act of singing becomes increasingly important the farther you go with voice training. If diaphragmatic-costal breathing works dependably for you, then the more sophisticated vocal techniques you want can also begin to work; if not, they probably won't, and your voice, like a foolish contractor's house, will fall down.

Figure 10.1 illustrates how important components of a singing performance relate to the supporting foundation provided by diaphragmatic-costal breathing. You can see that many of these are the very components that make singing interesting, expressive, and communicative—the qualities you want your singing to exhibit. As you try to develop these qualities, you will find that, unless you have started from a firmly controlled breathing habit, what you are trying to accomplish just won't happen.

Some singers, in their impatience to achieve expressive singing—because of a promising natural voice or great admiration for a successful singer whom they think they can imitate—tend to overlook the fundamental importance of developing disciplined breathing habits as the primary step. This will always lead to frustration and diminish their chances of reaching their vocal goals. The most direct route to the success they seek, whether it is great or modest, is the seemingly tedious path of mastering habitual breath control. That is the only way that allows the other components shown in Figure 10.1 to function as they should.

The diagram depicts a multiple-story structure to emphasize that building a voice is done by adding successive accomplishments, each dependent on the previous one for support, and all of them erected on a secure foundation of correct breathing habits. The ascending order of the

Figure 10.1. The Building of a Voice

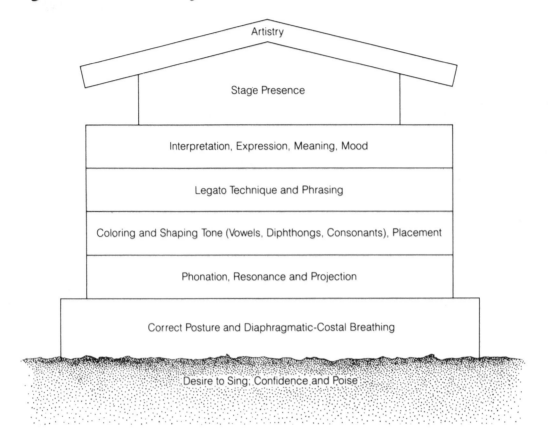

"floors" follows the suggested course of voice training outlined in the rest of this book, based on the assumption that the foundation, built first, will remain unshakable. As Step 1 discussed, the ground on which you build your voice is your desire to sing, prepared, smoothed out, and shaped by attitudes of confidence and poised assurance that you have developed. Then come the following:

Foundation	Habits of correct posture and diaphragmatic-costal breathing.
First Floor	Phonation: making tone, controlling its registers, adding resonance and projection.
Second Floor	Coloring and shaping the tone: formation of vowels, diphthongs, and consonants; forming words as meaningful successions of sounds; placement.
Third Floor	Development of legato technique: the smooth vocal line; phrasing.
Fourth Floor	Performance skills; working with audience response; refining vocal controls to eliminate specific performance faults.
Fifth Floor	Techniques of interpretation, expression, and meaning; mood, dynamics, and control of tempo.
Penthouse	Stage presence: the ultimate transformation of self-consciousness.
Roof	Artistry in singing: the crowning achievement that you would like others to hear every time you sing.

It is obvious that this diagram oversimplifies the voice-building process, but its most important message is the theme of this lesson: Success in singing is built upon secure breathing habits. It should be equally apparent that if you encounter continued difficulty with techniques on any of the "floors" listed, it may well be that some weakness in the breathing foundation remains uncorrected. Checking back to your habits of breathing may reveal the problem and allow you to put it right.

CLASS ACTIVITIES

Using Exercise 10.1 or 10.2 or a song designated by the instructor, the class will sing together, in small groups, and individually in one or more of the following ways. The aim is to relate your breathing processes to the way you meet specific challenges found in singing for others. Observe what you do to prepare and sustain the breath support required in each case. Some of these exercises involve techniques we have not yet explored, which will be studied in detail later in this book. For this activity simply use your present concept of what the particular type of singing calls for. This exploratory examination will lay a foundation for more thorough study later. Class discussion and critique of individual performances will be helpful for all.

1. Sing as if you were performing for a thousand people without a microphone. What do you have to do to project to that large an audience? Be specific: How did you breathe, modify posture, make tone, and so on?

2. Focus your attention on the exact vowel colors you sing. Are they accurate all the way through the song or exercise? Do they change when you run out of breath? On high notes? Can you make them more consistent by breathing more deeply?

3. Have listeners raise their hands every time they can't hear you make a consonant clearly. If several hands come up, sing the word again, trying to make every consonant completely audible so that hands don't come up. Notice what you do with breathing and tone to make this happen.

4. Sing the song or exercise using one of the moods in Class Activity 2 of Lesson 4 (p. 11). Observe how you breathe to project the mood you choose. Don't tell your listeners what mood you are using; then ask them what mood they got from your singing.

5. Gradually and evenly get louder from beginning to end; then reverse the process, going from loud to soft. Notice where you feel the control of the process: Is it in the throat or lower down? Does putting the control above the waistline help you accomplish more even dynamic changes?

6. Sing each phrase on one breath without breaking the flow of tone. Exaggerate the smoothness of the vocal line. Can you make all the tones have the same degree of loudness and intensity from beginning to end? Can you sing the entire song or exercise as a succession of such smooth phrases? How does this affect the way you breathe?

Exercise 10.1.   Transpose up and down.

Exercise 10.2.   Breathe only at the beginning and at breathing marks. Don't *let yourself* breathe anywhere else in the line. (*Note:* The entire song is in the Song Collection, p. 260.)

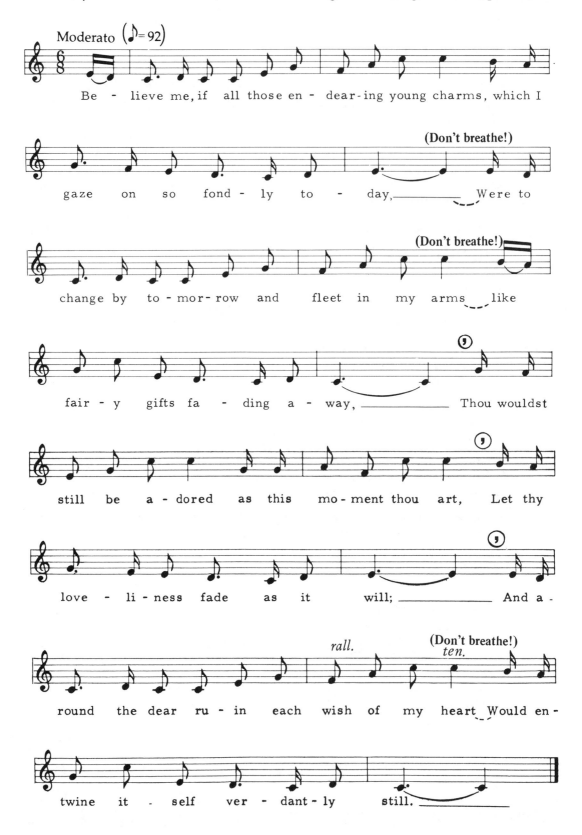

ON YOUR OWN

As you walk along, inhale in a diaphragmatic-costal manner for exactly six steps, completely filling your lungs. Then completely exhale on the following six steps. Do this several times so that you get a feeling of completely filling and emptying your lungs in a fixed time. When six counts are secure, successively lengthen the count to seven, eight, nine, ten, etc. It's not as simple as it sounds! Be sure that you walk in as much of a singing posture as you can and that all your breathing is deep.

Making Tone

Singing means making sustained vocal sounds on pitch. These sounds are the products of the phonation machine, and we understand them as *tone*. By itself, tone is simply the raw material of singing; it must be shaped, controlled, and given expressive colors if singing is to have meaning. Step 3 examines the various kinds of tone your voice can make and how the sounds are produced, amplified, and controlled to make what we identify as singing tone.

CONTENTS OF STEP 3

LESSON 11

On Opening Up

CONCEPTS

Yawn. That's it—wide open, nice and easy and relaxed.

Feel good? Of course. That's what a yawn is for—to let you relax, breathe deeply, and stretch muscles comfortably. One of its principal features is the wide-open position of the mouth, which is coupled with an easing of tension in the jaw and throat muscles. If you were biting into a thick hamburger you might open your jaw just as wide, but since you would expect some resistance from the food, you would tense those muscles instead. Notice that the feeling of a real yawn relaxes them.

Now yawn again. When you are wide open and have breathed deeply, say "Ahhhh . . . " as though you were thoroughly enjoying yourself. Prolong it a little, using a rising and falling inflection. This ought to feel even better than the first yawn because it combines the pleasant sensation of making tone with the comfort of the yawn. Notice that the tone you make in saying "Ah" comes easily, almost as though it were part of the yawn itself.

Now yawn one more time, and this time *sing:*

If you didn't change the position you used for saying "Ah," your singing should have felt good too. In both speaking and singing, the yawn position eliminates muscular tension in the throat and encourages you to breathe deeply. These are the conditions that are essential for resonant phonation, or what most singers would call *making good tone.*

You obviously would not want to sing all the notes of a song in the wide-open-jaw, yawn position, but using it as a beginning device to make tone helps you experience for yourself the *feeling* of open, strain-free, deeply supported phonation. The tone you make in this position may now feel different from your normal singing tone—perhaps uncontrolled, raw, even blatant to begin with—but don't dismiss it too quickly. Increased familiarity with it will reveal its usefulness in helping to expand your concepts of tone production. The most notable characteristics of this tone production are worth listing:

1. It is *open.* The yawn position assures that.

2. It has *deep breath support*. Yawning involves breathing deeply.

3. It gives tone making a *feeling of freedom*. The yawn position keeps possible obstructions—the tongue, soft palate, teeth, and lips—out of the way.

4. It gives you the *physical sensation* that tone making results directly from deep breath support in coordination with an open throat. *This is the key to further progress.*

Every tone you sing should have deep breath support, be free from strain, and have the open resonance that starts with room in the throat. If these qualities are not present, you are forced to make tone by working against the natural functioning of your phonation machine. It is imperative that you develop an awareness of when the process is working right and when it isn't.

Probably you now find that some vowels are harder to sing than others and that, when you try to sing them, you close your throat or mouth, weaken your breath support, sing a throaty sound, or strain in some manner. To overcome these problems you need to realize that all vowels *can* be made in an open-throat position, with deep support. Then you must begin to find out how to carry over the feeling of openness and support you felt in the yawn position into singing vowels other than "Ah."

Notice that we did *not* say that all the vowels must be made with the *jaw* wide open, although that too is possible to a remarkable extent. But it is necessary to keep the *throat* open even though the jaw is not stretched. You need to discover positions that will allow this to happen for all the vowels. Step 4 will examine the exact formation of all of the vowels.

Just as breathing correctly can happen only when the body is in correct singing posture, the central activity of singing—making tone, or phonation—can function well only when those parts of your phonation machine we called the vibrator in Figure 6.1 remain in their natural, unstrained positions. An added difficulty is that these parts cannot be seen, or even felt, necessarily, in the way you can check your feet, chest, and shoulders for posture. The yawn position at the beginning of this lesson is a good reference point from which to begin refining your concepts of tone, because it makes you start with the one essential characteristic that tones must have: openness.

CLASS ACTIVITIES

1. Put two or three fingers on edge between your front teeth. Relax your jaw and throat muscles as you did to yawn; don't bite a hamburger! Now sing Exercise 11.1, trying to maintain the yawn feeling throughout. When it seems to work that way, sing it another time, tensing all those muscles as though you were biting. (Keep your fingers between your teeth for this.) Observe what you have changed. Can you *feel* where the changes happen? Notice the difference they make in the tone quality.

2. Take the fingers out of your mouth, and, keeping as much of your jaw and mouth position as you can, sing the exercise on OH. Can you sing so that you have the same feeling as the AH in Activity 1, and the only thing you change is the vowel color? The tone should feel pretty much the same, made in the same place, with the same support and freedom. If you tighten anything to change the vowel, try to isolate what you do.

3. On successive performances sing the vowels AW, UH, EH, IH, and EE. You may experience increasing difficulty in keeping the tone open and deeply supported. Try to discover what it is you feel you have to change to make the new vowel. Are you closing up, straining, eliminating breath support? When you discover a specific fault, can you then sing the vowel in a way that does not let the fault happen?

4. Sing a familiar song on the vowel AH in the yawn position. Can you maintain the open position all the way through every phrase? If not, why do you change? What are the difficulties?

One of the greatest values of these activities is that they allow each class member to observe others trying to meet the demands of the exercise. Watching someone else solve the problem can help you to work your own solution out.

Exercise 11.1.

AH_____
OH_____
(Add other vowels.)

ON YOUR OWN

Under a good light in front of your mirror, yawn and sing a song or phrase on a wide-open AH. As you sing, can you see the back wall of your throat in the mirror? Discover what you have to do to keep the tongue flat enough, and the soft palate high enough, to allow you to see it clearly while you are making tone. When you start to sing, does your throat start to close up? Does your tongue rise? Can you find out why you feel you have to do this closing-up process and how you could make tone without having it happen?

LESSON 12

What Is a "Beautiful" Tone?

CONCEPTS

How many different sounds can your voice make?

You are constantly answering that question in the various ways you use your voice. You talk, yell, sigh, shout, scream, sob, laugh, moan, cry—even sing. In singing the question becomes more refined: "How many sounds can your voice *control*?" Singing depends on control of phonation— the firm management of sustained vocal sounds on pitch in ways that convey meaning and emotion.

Think about what you now do to exercise such control over your singing sounds. One of the most basic control mechanisms is your concept of the "best" tone you can produce, the tone you want to sing most. What is it? What qualities does that "best," "ideal," "perfect" tone have? Is it "beautiful," "pleasing," or "good"? When you are sounding particularly fine in the shower, what is it that makes the sound so satisfying? How do you control the differences between those tones and other tones you may sing that aren't so rewarding?

You may feel that so far *none* of the sounds you have sung have been all that fine. But think about it. That simply means you have decided that something else is better. What is it? Specifically, how does it contrast with the sounds you now make that do not please you?

As you explore these questions, it will become apparent that terms such as *good, ideal,* and *perfect* don't describe very much in themselves. We often use them to point at some quality that words will not quite explain. However, serious and comparative exploration of the singing sounds you make will bring into your vocabulary more precise words to help explain specific qualities of tone. *Resonant, supported, unstrained, breathy, throaty, swallowed,* and other such terms designate specific qualities of sound that can be observed and controlled. When you understand such terms, and have found out what you do to produce—or avoid—the tones they describe, your concepts of "beautiful" and "ideal" tone will probably have become clearer also.

What, after all, *is* "beautiful"? Some people object to using the word because they think it implies sentimentality or artificiality or applies only to kinds of music they don't care for. Yet they would hardly set out to sing "ugly," "dull," or "uninteresting" sounds, so they must have some concept of the tones they consider valuable.

The dictionary defines *beauty* as "the quality that gives pleasure to the senses or pleasurably exalts the mind or spirit; loveliness. . . ." By this explanation, any singing that gives pleasure could be called beautiful, but when the term is applied to tone it generally means a more limited group of sounds that have recognizable qualities of openness, deep support, clarity, resonance, accuracy of pitch, and emotional coloring. Those terms are specific in that they describe tonal characteristics that can be identified separately and controlled by conscious effort.

If you have ever gone into a restaurant and smelled food cooking, you can understand the subtle differences that make exact definition of *beautiful* so difficult. What is the difference, in precise terms, between food smells that make you think, "That's greasy!" and those that whet your appetite because they are so enticing? Words fail to explain it, yet you are instantly aware of which ones you are smelling. So it is with beauty; you may not be able to describe it, but you can certainly recognize it.

It is just this elusive quality about beauty of tone that you need to think about and begin to build into the concepts that control your tone production. You may now use *beautiful, ideal,* or even *good* to designate the kind of tone you most want to sing, without really being able to say exactly what they mean. The path to giving those terms real meaning lies through the study of qualities of tone that can be identified and examined, such as those mentioned above. The starting point is the quality of tone that the phonation machine produces in its most natural, vital, and unstrained position. On this you need to build singing habits that do not let strain, poor breath support, or any sort of constriction of muscles interfere with the development of a tone that demonstrates what *beautiful* means to you.

CLASS ACTIVITIES

Activities for this lesson employ a device called *the tonal continuum* (Figure 12.1), which provides a convenient means of exploring differences among qualities of tone. It represents graphically the total range of sounds your voice can make, between opposing extremes of "bad" sound which involve strain and distorted production and which you probably don't regard as singing. Midway between these is the area of what you consider your "ideal" or "best" tone quality, the one you want to use for singing. The fact that the same mechanism produces all of these sounds demonstrates the great flexibility of that mechanism and, more importantly, that you do have clear, conscious control over the kinds of sounds you produce for any given meaning or use.

1. Make sounds on various vowels at both ends of the continuum. If you can, sing them on a uniform pitch, but exaggerate the extreme nature of the sound. It should be what is usually known as "bad" sound. The class will sing together first, and then individuals will be asked to illustrate their own concepts.

2. Using similar vowels, sing what you consider to be your own "ideal" tone—first as a class, then individually.

3. Analyze what you do, mentally and physically, to make the difference between "bad" tone and "ideal" tone. Where do you feel each tone? Does your posture, breathing, or muscular tension have anything to do with it? What other factors can you identify?

Figure 12.1.   The Tonal Continuum

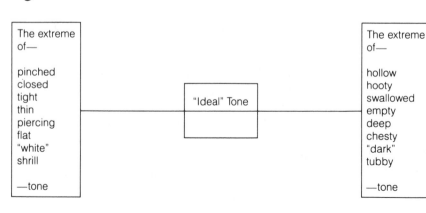

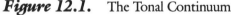

4. The class will be divided into groups. Each group will sing Exercises 12.1 and 12.2, using what they feel to be their "ideal" tone quality. The rest of the class will judge where along the continuum that tone actually falls, both for the sound of the whole group and for any individual voices that stand out. Does the tone fall in the area that the class feels is in the "ideal" region on the graph? Does it sound too much like one of the extremes? In successive repetitions, observe what happens to the "ideal" quality when high and low notes, or loud and soft notes, are sung. If different vowels are used, do some of them seem to produce more of the "ideal" quality than do others?

5. Using a song you have learned or one of the exercises, sing with a consistent tone quality that falls somewhere between the "ideal" area and one of the extremes. Contrast its feeling and sound with your "ideal" tone. Can you maintain that quality consistently as long as you keep your attention on it? Try to compile a list (either by class discussion or by personal assignment) of specific things that happen when you produce particular qualities. For example, the blatant, pinched extreme may make the jaw and throat tight, breathing shallow, and tones feel nasal and strained.

Exercise 12.1. Transpose up and down.

Exercise 12.2. The instructor may change the words to use other vowels.

ON YOUR OWN

1. Go back to your mirror. Repeat the tonal continuum exercises for yourself. Notice your physical appearance as you produce each kind of tone. Identify differences in posture, breathing, and the positions of the jaw, mouth, throat, and chest. Does your "ideal" tone quality improve if you assume better posture? If you pay more attention to the open quality discussed in Lesson 11?

2.   Listen to some famous singers whose names your instructor can suggest. For this exercise, concentrate on singers of the serious music styles, watching them on television, if possible. Even though the music or language may be unfamiliar to you, pay close attention to the vocal sounds the singers make, evaluating them in terms of the tonal continuum concepts. Do the singers ever use sounds at the extremes of the continuum? How would you describe the differences between their "ideal" sounds and yours?

LESSON 13

Controlling Your Registers

CONCEPTS

Does your voice "crack," "break," or lose power on certain notes?

Don't feel there's something wrong if that happens; such cracking is perfectly normal and demonstrates that your voice is working as it is built to do. Another automobile analogy will be useful. When you accelerate, your engine must shift from gear to gear in order to use its power efficiently at various speeds. This shifting involves a break in even acceleration; an automatic transmission takes care of the shifting for you and makes the transitions as smooth as possible, but shifts made by hand produce more of a jolt.

Every normal voice moves through various "gears" called *registers*. A register is one segment of your total range in which your voice operates in a uniform, coordinated way. The vocal folds produce the tones of the register with very little change of position. At the top and bottom of the register, differences in vibration rate—faster for high tones and slower for low tones—necessitate changing to a different position, or mode of production, much as your car shifts gears. An actual adjustment of the vocal folds takes place.

Your voice has an "automatic transmission" at these points, and it works very smoothly if you allow it to. Attempts to "shift by hand"—that is, to force changes by muscular tension or strain—defeat the automatic function completely. Poor posture, weak breath support, and throat tension interfere with the process by upsetting its natural, balanced operation. Attempts to force a register out of its normal range by singing it too high or too low are like trying to drive at seventy-five miles per hour in low gear, and this can do real damage to the apparatus.

Remember, registers are normal components of the phonation process. They are built into your voice, so to achieve the control of singing you are working toward you need to identify them and learn to use them effectively. Here are some useful steps in accomplishing this.

1. *Locate the "breaks" in your voice.* Figure 13.1 shows the approximate range of the registers in men's and women's voices. Breaks are likely to occur in the areas where the registers overlap, although the woman's voice has them in other segments of the scale as well. You should locate and mark the exact notes on the staff where your voice has the greatest tendency to break or lose power and clarity. Knowing this will help you when you sing songs, because you will be better prepared to sing melodies containing those notes in ways that will minimize the effect of the break.

2. *Observe what your voice normally does at those breaks.* Do you strain, yell, tighten up, make a throaty sound, sound breathy, or even stop singing? You become aware that you are not able to

Figure 13.1. Registers of the Singing Voice

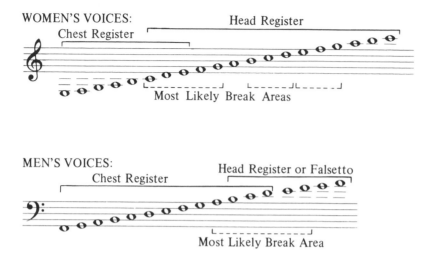

sing your ideal tone, and this may make you afraid even to try certain notes. Yet you realize that, if you are going to sing the whole song, you have to do *something* in order to keep singing. What is that something? If it now involves strain or distortion of your phonation apparatus, can you discover another way to produce the tone that avoids the problems? Remember, the aim is to let the "automatic transmission" of your voice do the necessary shifting into a register position that will produce the tone without forcing or straining.

3. *Identify and learn to use two principal registers of your voice.* Every voice has at least two. They are usually called *chest* and *head* registers, perhaps because the physical sensations produced by their tones are felt most in those areas. Women normally sing mostly in the head register, while men's voices lie for the most part in the chest register. The most important thing to realize, however, is that *all voices have both registers, and the best singing draws on the benefits of both of them.*

When your tone breaks, it is simply shifting, rather roughly, into another register. If your habit now is to strain or force tones at the top or bottom of a register shown on Figure 13.1, try to discover a new way to sing those tones without straining. That new way may use a tone production you do not now think of as singing, but try it anyway. Your instructor will supervise these attempts, and you can compare your voice with others in the class with similar problems.

More intensive voice training will reveal subdivisions of the two principal registers, but for now you should be concerned principally with the chest and head registers. The ultimate aim in controlling registers is to strengthen the automatic nature of their operation. This has been called *fusion of the registers,* which suggests a balanced operation that allows you to pass back and forth between them without cracking. This can happen only when the principal registers are about equal in strength and independence. The first step toward such fusion may be to isolate and strengthen your "other" register—the one you now don't use very much. For women this is the pure *chest tone,* and for men (at least at the outset) it is the *falsetto.*

The Woman's Chest Tone

The woman's voice can produce a pure chest tone of great power and depth, especially on the tones from middle C downward. It is a tone very similar to that sung by a baritone. While most women can sing those notes with a type of head tone, real power and ease are found only by singing them with a chest tone. This permits the relaxation of throat muscles that builds strength into the entire phonation process and ordinarily carries over to some extent into production of tones in the head register. Some women tend to shy away from this tone quality as unfeminine or too mannish, but they must realize that it is a vital, normal part of the voice's construction, which will add power and projection to the entire voice. Some of the exercises given in the Class Activities for this lesson will help you isolate the quality.

The Man's Falsetto

The purest form of head register tone in the man's voice is called *falsetto,* as indicated in Figure 13.1. Some men want to reject this as a childish sound that they outgrew at puberty, but it too is a normal part of the way the voice operates. It is simply the voice most men used as children, and it is still available to be used as a source of ease and clarity in singing. It is the basis for what later will become the true head tone of the man's voice—a light, floating quality of upper tones that results from controlled blending of falsetto with the strength of the chest register. Most men have a pronounced vocal break somewhere just above middle C. Many of the severe problems this presents to them can be quickly eased by the rather simple process of singing pure falsetto in the interval of a sixth above the break. The tones of this singing should be clear, strain-free, and virtually effortless. See the exercises given in the Class Activities.

CLASS ACTIVITIES

The following exercises will be sung by the entire class, by women's and men's voices separately, and particularly by individuals so that personal difficulties may be examined. Repeat each exercise enough times to reveal both the problems and some possible solutions. Record the singing for playback and class critique if possible. The exercises are aimed at developing an ability to control the "other" registers—the woman's chest tone and the man's falsetto. Tones produced should be:

1. clear, resonant, and not breathy;

2. produced completely in the right register, without mixtures from the other register;

3. produced without strain or unusual muscular effort;

4. controlled by the singer experiencing the specific sensation of producing tone in that register and singing it deliberately rather than by accident.

1. *Exercises for all voices.*

Exercise 13.1.

a. Men will sing Exercise 13.1 as written, with an open, easy AH vowel.
b. Women will sing the exercise, matching what the men sang. Sing *the same sound,* with exactly the same pitches and vowel color (not an octave higher). Use the yawn position of Lesson 11, eliminating tension from the throat and jaw. *Let* the tone happen.
c. The whole class will sing it together, striving for one uniform sound. (Women sing chest tone.)

Exercise 13.2.

d. Women will sing Exercise 13.2 as written, with a clear, round, OO vowel.

e. Men will sing *the same sound* (not an octave lower), in falsetto, matching the women's tone. Relax the throat completely, and try to eliminate fuzziness.

f. The entire class will sing it together, making one uniform sound.

Exercise 13.3.

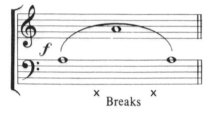

g. All voices will sing Exercise 13.3 together, trying consciously to insert vocal breaks between lower and upper tones as indicated by the *x*'s. Produce all three tones at the same volume and without sliding pitches.

2. *Exercises for women's voices.*

Exercise 13.4.

a. Women will sing Exercise 13.4. Start with the chest tone used in Exercise 13.1 and break over into the head register where indicated by the *x*. This should be an audible break, much like yodeling.

Exercise 13.5.

b. Women will sing Exercise 13.5, first singing all notes in head tone. Do *not* break over even if you feel as though you should. Then sing again, and change to chest tone sharply on the note marked *x*. Try to increase the ease and openness of the tones following the change.

Exercise 13.6.

AH——————————— AH——————————— AH———————
OH——————————— OH——————————— OH———————

c.   Women will first try to sing Exercise 13.6 entirely with head tone. Follow the notation as you sing, and mark the exact note where you feel loss of power or a need to break to chest tone. The second time, sing the entire exercise *forte* (*f*). Start with head tone and, at the tone you marked, change to chest tone, maintaining the loud dynamic.

3.   *Exercises for men's voices.*

Exercise 13.7.

AH ——————————————————————

a.   Men will first sing Exercise 13.7 with chest tone. You will probably have to yell for the last two or three notes; be sure you keep as deep a breath support as possible. As you sing, mark the note at which you feel the tone should break over into falsetto. The second time, sing the entire exercise with an even, moderately loud tone, breaking over into falsetto at the note you marked. Try to sing the falsetto tones clearly and without breathiness. (For most voices the last two or possibly three notes will be easier if sung falsetto.)

Exercise 13.8.

OO

b.   Men will sing Exercise 13.8 entirely in falsetto. Use a hootlike tone, with a clear, unbreathy OO vowel. Aim for the sound a child might make imitating a train whistle. Relax the throat and jaw as completely as you can. If the tone is clear, you may feel as though it were vibrating near the bridge of your nose.

ON YOUR OWN

1.   Sing some of the Class Activity exercises before your mirror. If you had trouble making chest tone or falsetto, watch what you are tensing up as you sing, which may be preventing the tone from being clear; then try to sing the tones again and not let that tension start.

2.   Hear a singer in live performance; serious styles are preferable because they usually present more vocal demands in the area of register control. As you watch and listen, try to observe what the singer does, or fails to do, in controlling registers and using them to advantage in interpretation. Do women sing easily only in chest tone and have to work and strain to sing head tones? Or is their chest tone so weak or undeveloped that they have to force and push to sing lower notes? Can men sing high notes only by shouting or tightening up, or have they learned to use the ease and clarity of the falsetto?

LESSON 14

Making Your Ideal Tone

CONCEPTS

In Lesson 12 we asked you to sing what you felt was your ideal tone. You were not asked to define it or explain it—just sing it. The objective was to provide sharp contrast to what was obviously bad tone of various sorts, so practically any tone was an improvement. That experience may have led you to examine the nature of the tone you would most like to have your voice produce.

Now that we have considered some of the fundamentals of the voice's operation, we can begin to examine the nature of ideal tone—yours or anyone else's. Your own will have certain unique characteristics that spring from your individual personality. When you hear great singers perform, the presence of such personal traits is usually obvious in their singing. In short, they sound like themselves. In addition, however, some of their greatness results from the fact that they sing tones that can be understood objectively as fine, rich, correctly produced, beautiful— even "ideal"—and their singing can be appreciated precisely because the quality of the sounds they make has an independent value and attractiveness.

We have examined some characteristics of such tones, and the remaining steps in this book will take up others in detail. In considering an ideal tone quality we are not just pointing at some vague, emotional goal such as "beautiful singing." Instead we are urging you to build on your present concepts of value and quality in tone. This is a specific procedure, involving answers to questions about what such tone is, how you make it, how you learn to use it consistently and avoid other kinds of tone, and how it relates to your concepts of expressiveness in singing. Tone is the singer's principal product; its quality is of the greatest importance to singing success. Here are some characteristics of ideal tone:

Five Qualities of Ideal Tone

1. *Ideal tone always has deep breath support and sounds like it.* As we pointed out in Step 2, every tone is the direct result of deep, controlled breathing. Dependable tone can be made in no other way.

2. *Ideal tone sounds and feels open and free from strain.* Lesson 11 stressed the importance of this characteristic of tone making. Muscles of the throat, neck, jaw, and lips are never rigid but rather work in a flexible and unstrained manner. The normal physical effort of singing is never allowed to interfere with the operation of these muscles.

3. *Ideal tone is accurate.* Much later in this book (Lesson 26), we will examine what is involved in accurate singing in the broadest sense. Many elements in addition to tone making are involved, especially in expressive singing. In applying the term only to the production of tone, we focus on at least two specific attributes of tone itself: pitch and vowel color. The former must be exact and unwavering, the latter correct and consistent. Step 4 examines the subtle ways in which faulty or lazy vowel production can erode even a well-produced tone. For the present it is crucial that you become sensitive to slight variations of pitch, such as flatting, sharping, or sliding, and train yourself to hear whether the vowel color you produce is the one actually called for by the word you are singing.

4. *Ideal tone has a feeling of forward placement.* This concept will be explored in Lesson 19. For the present, note that forward placement produces the physical sensation that tone is focused under the bridge of the nose. For this reason it is often called *singing in the mask.* This can be achieved only by tone that is deeply supported, open, free from tension, and resonated to the fullest. This must not be confused with nasal tone, which is made by blocking or pinching the sound and preventing nasal resonance. The most nasal tone you can make is produced by simply holding your nose to sing or using the soft palate to close off the nasal passage at the back. Such tone can give a feeling of vibration in the nose, but it is the opposite of forward placement because it is a blockage rather than an opening.

5. *Ideal tone produces a feeling of tonal control.* It gives you the sensation that you can shape every tone, using precisely the color, power, and expression you wish. You become physically aware that this is because everything is working right: "All systems are go!" It is a sensation much like that of driving a new luxury car that "handles like a dream" and does everything you want it to. Because all of the car's systems are working as they should, you have the feeling of easy control. As your singing begins to produce more "ideal" tones than "clinkers," this analogy will become increasingly meaningful.

Great singers habitually sing phrases and whole songs in which virtually every tone has these five characteristics. Notes flow on, one to the next, in a richly consistent quality. This level of singing performance is so essential and recognizable that it has been given a name: *legato technique.* Lesson 21 goes into detail about its requirements. When you hear music sung by competent singers with this technique, differences from your own tone production may become clearer. While you may sing individual tones that have the five qualities listed, chances are that in between are tones that are noticeably faulty.

The first steps toward legato technique involve producing controlled ideal tones consciously and singing them in succession so that the tone quality does not falter or break down.

CLASS ACTIVITIES

Learn Exercise 14.1 thoroughly for frequent class and individual use. Using it as a warm-up over several successive class meetings will be valuable both as a vocal exercise and as continued training in the concepts of this lesson. To begin, use the exercise in the following ways:

1.   The class, and then each individual, will sing Note 1 with the best (most ideal) tone possible. Refer to the five qualities listed in the Concepts. Compare individuals' tones on the basis of those qualities. If possible, record each person's singing of Note 1, and play it back before proceeding.

2.   When Note 1 can be sung securely, begin adding notes, one at a time, always starting with Note 1 (1–2, 1–2–3, 1–2–3–4, etc.). Focus all your attention on whether the initial tone quality can be carried on. If it cannot, what changes? Can you hear and feel the change when it happens? Can you then sing the progression without the change? The ultimate aim is to sing Notes 1–7 (the first phrase), breathe, and proceed to Notes 8–15 with no change of quality, using the vowel colors indicated (or others suggested by the instructor). In striving for this objective, notice what prevents your reaching it. Use the following list of common problems as a guide:

a.   Do you run out of breath? Why? Poor posture, shallow breathing, breathy or throaty tone?

b.   Are your throat, jaw, lips, or tongue tense?

c.   Are you singing the wrong vowel color? Say the word naturally, and compare it with the sound you are singing.

d.   Do you insert "H" sounds before certain notes? Why?

e.   Are you afraid of high tones and thus tighten up or change the vowel?

f.   Do you have uncontrolled register breaks?

Exercise 14.1.

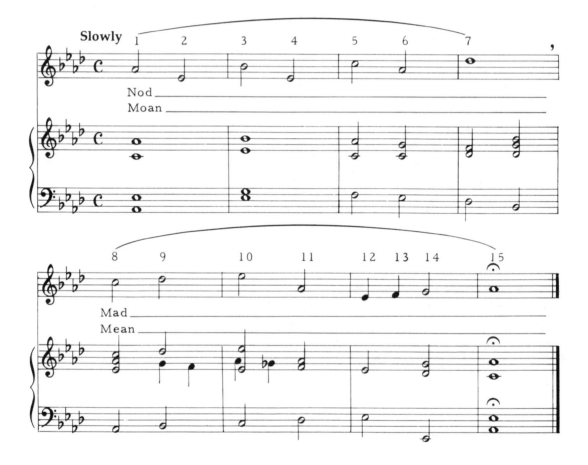

ON YOUR OWN

1.   Sing Exercise 14.1 repeatedly over a period of days and weeks. Record it for playback several times to note your progress. Remember anything the instructor or class may have suggested about what you did in class in your attempt to incorporate the five characteristics of ideal tone. Try increasingly not to let yourself sing *any* tone that doesn't have those qualities.

2.   Watch yourself in the mirror, wearing as few clothes as your modesty will permit, to locate mistakes of posture, muscular strain, lack of adequate opening, and so on. Sing Exercise 14.1 and songs on which you are working.

LESSON 15

Resonance and Projection

CONCEPTS

Resonance looks something like *re-sound*. In singing, resonance describes how the sounds made by the vocal folds are built up, in a process that could be called *re-sounding them*.

The process requires space, which is available only in the throat (pharynx), mouth, and nasal passages. If such space is not provided, tones sound thick, muffled, covered, colorless, or sometimes thin and pinched. It is hardly logical to expect the small vocal folds, by themselves, to produce the wide range of vocal sounds—from sighs to shouts—of which your voice is capable. Something more is needed; the original sounds must be amplified, intensified, and made richer. This is what resonance does.

The Echo

An echo is an understandable analogy. You shout in a canyon; the sound travels about 1,100 feet per second and bounces off the opposite side. How soon you will hear it again depends on how far the sound must travel. If the canyon wall is 550 feet away, you hear the echo in about one second. If it then bounces off the wall behind you and continues bouncing, you hear successive echoes about every second, getting gradually softer each time. In a sense, you are hearing the same sound over and over, because the sound waves are trapped in the canyon, reverberating back and forth. The fact that the canyon walls have the right shape allows the original sound to be multiplied, or re-sounded.

Compress this concept into your singing. Your vocal folds set up vibrations in the spaces of your throat, mouth, and nasal passages. A similar bouncing and trapping process takes place, but the distance is so small that the reverberations happen several hundred times a second. When the sound comes out of your head, all the reverberations are heard as part of the original sound in a fraction of a second. The tone has been "re-sounded," or resonated.

It is obvious that, when the space for this re-sounding is constricted or eliminated, the process won't work very well. Not all canyons have echoes; but those that do must have the right shape and space to make echoes possible. Similarly, if you don't shape your resonating spaces correctly—particularly your throat and mouth—you won't get much re-sounding either. This is already clear to you in a very common way; when your nose is stuffed up by a cold, your singing tone sounds muffled and obstructed.

You cannot alter the physical process by which sound is resonated, but you can affect your resonance by being sure that the maximum, correct space is available for it. Here are two characteristics of fully resonated tone that can be both heard and physically experienced:

1. *A resonated tone sounds open, clear, and free from tension.* It is bright, focused, and not marred by breathiness, throatiness, or a fuzzy quality. It rings.

2. *A resonated tone has a quality of warmth and richness.* This quality is usually described in terms with emotional, expressive connotations, probably because the process of resonation adds dimensions of sound that go beyond the basics of pitch and loudness. These dimensions give the tone a unique *timbre,* or specific quality, just as an orchestral instrument has a distinctive sound that distinguishes it from all other instruments.

Projection

The addition of resonance to tone increases its ability to carry, or have "projection." This makes your singing fill a room, be heard easily and naturally, and have the fullest range of expression.

You are familiar with projection in speaking, because you do it automatically in many situations. Speaking to someone right next to you requires little projection, because you know subconsciously that the tone does not have to carry very far. However, if you speak to someone across a large room you raise your voice—that is, you speak more loudly and with greater intensity. This intensity involves added resonance, which is the quality that makes the tone project across the greater distance. When you want to attract someone's attention at a great distance, you shout. If the shouting is pinched or hurts your throat, the other person probably won't hear you, since you have eliminated resonance and the sound will not project very well. By shouting with deep support and a wide opening, you increase resonance, you don't hurt your throat, and you make your friend hear you.

This whole process applies to singing. By being sure your tone has its maximum resonance, you ensure that your audience will hear you and that the tone will be secure and rich in quality. A rule of thumb in performance is to sing to the person farthest from you, to apply the habit of projecting in terms of the space you have to fill with sound.

You may have noticed a close correlation between the requirements for resonance and projection and the open, ideal tonal requirements discussed in Lessons 11 and 14. This is not accidental. *The open, ideal tone is richly resonant and, as a result, projects easily and well.*

CLASS ACTIVITIES

Use Exercises 15.1 and 15.2 (p. 62) in the following ways:

1. While you are singing with the class, ask yourself the questions listed below, as you produce the different kinds of tone requested. Compare what you are doing with what you hear others singing around you.

    a. Sing with a completely unresonant tone.

        1. What do you do to produce that effect?

        2. Do you tighten or close your throat, strain, or make a nasal sound?

b. Repeat, and add more resonance than you normally use.
   1. Is this tone like the "dark" end of the tonal continuum (p. 48)?
   2. Does it help to sing in the yawn position (p. 44)?
   3. Do you find yourself breathing more deeply to make this tone?
c. Sing Activities a and b again, using the vowels EE (me) and IH (bit).
   1. Do you tighten up more than on AH? Why?
   2. Do these vowels make it harder to add resonance from a to b? Why?

2. Individuals will perform all of Activity 1 as solos for the class. If possible, the instructor will record and play these performances back for everyone. Then the class will hold a general discussion to point out each person's strengths and weaknesses. This procedure takes time, but it is essential that each person actually *hear* what sounds he or she makes; this is most helpful when students can make immediate comparisons with others' performances. The objective is to help each person explore the meaning of resonance in personal tone making, by actually experimenting with the sounds needed to produce it. This cannot really be done by theory alone; it must involve the sounds themselves.

3. In a large classroom or an auditorium, one singer goes on stage or to one side of the room, while the class is at a distance. Using Exercises 15.1 and 15.2 or a familiar song, the singer tries to project it across the room so that the class hears it clearly. Whenever they cannot hear well, or understand the words, students raise their hands. The singer's challenge is to sing through the song with no hands being raised. Have a general class evaluation of each performance, concerning the following:

   a. Did the singer try to project only by straining, screaming, or making a pinched, harsh tone?

   b. What special tonal problems prevented the singer's voice from carrying? Breathy tone? Thin, weak quality? Closed mouth and jaw? Pinched or flattened vowel sounds?

   c. As specifically as possible, point out what the singer did to correct the problem when hands were raised.

Exercise 15.1.

Exercise 15.2.

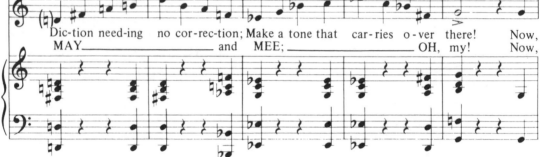
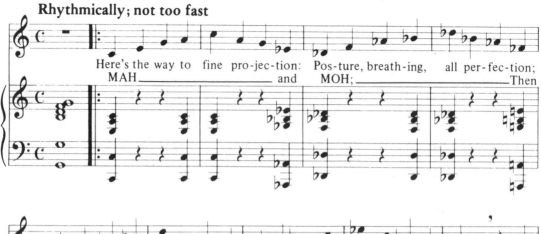

Rhythmically; not too fast

Here's the way to fine pro-jec-tion: Pos-ture, breath-ing, all per-fec-tion;
MAH_____ and MOH;_____Then

Dic-tion need-ing no cor-rec-tion; Make a tone that car-ries o-ver there! Now,
MAY_____ and MEE;_____OH, my! Now,

sing it a-gain!_____ Oh! this is the end!_____

ON YOUR OWN

Experiment—a little, and when your neighbors won't protest—with how you shout. First, open to the yawn position, breathe deeply, and shout "HAH!" prolonging it some. You should feel as though the tone were "coming up from the floor"—a sensation of deep support for a wide-open sound that may produce some feeling of vibration in the chest.

Next, shout "HEY!" once or twice, but pinch it, making it shrill and tight. This should produce a feeling of obstruction in your throat, and, since it can be hard on your tone-making apparatus, don't do it more than once or twice.

Which of these two shouts uses tone most like what you want to sing? The answer should be obvious. Remember, the shout is using the same mechanism for tone making that singing does.

Coloring Tone

When your breathing habits become secure enough so that you can produce controlled singing tone consistently, you are ready to begin shaping the tone so that it conveys the meaning of the words and music. This involves *coloring* the tone, by giving it the specific sound values of vowels and diphthongs and by inserting consonants into the singing line to create understandable words. The art of *placement* allows you to sing a sequence of correctly shaped sounds, thus creating a continuous and meaningful vocal line. This step examines the tonal shapes used in singing English and relates them to the correct breathing and resonant phonation we have been examining in the first three steps.

CONTENTS OF STEP 4

LESSON 16

Are You a Kansas Yankee from Birmingham?

CONCEPTS

When someone speaks with an accent, what are they *doing* to make that distinctive sound?

Various regions of the United States—the South, New England, Texas, the Midwest, the Far West—are known for typical speech patterns that we call *accents* or *dialects*. People from other countries, for whom English is a second language, often make English sounds in unique ways because those sounds do not occur in their native languages.

An accent is a distinctive way of *coloring* sounds—pronouncing vowels and articulating consonants. Since vowels are the major components of tone, and consonants divide tone into words, their coloring affects the entire flow of sound, and we are very aware of it. This is especially true when it differs from our own.

Singing demands an even more controlled coloring of tone than speaking. When you sing a word, you sustain the vowels longer than you would in speaking. If you are giving them wrong colors, mistakes are magnified because you are prolonging them. To avoid such problems you must have an exact, detailed knowledge of how every vowel is made, and a well-established habit of producing the same color for a given vowel each time.

Wrong vowel colors and poorly articulated consonants weaken your attempts to make ideal tone quality, just as a flat tire disrupts the operation of your car. You may be doing many other things right, but if your listeners hear wrong vowels, all of your singing sounds faulty. Remember, singing is a single, unified act; coloring tone is one of its basic components, which must work in coordination with everything else to produce the desired result.

Before we begin to study vowels and consonants in detail, here are three basic principles about coloring sound. They apply equally to speaking and to singing. You can hear them working when you listen to singers and speakers whom you cannot understand or whose tone annoys you.

Three Principles of Tone-Coloring

1. *Accurate vowel color produces pure tone quality.* If we ask you to sing "beautiful, rich tone," you may wonder exactly what we want, because *beautiful* is too general a term to make clear the differences in the sounds you sing. But vowel colors are more specific. If you feel that your tone isn't beautiful, the first thing to check on is the vowel color you are producing. Are you making

one consistent, accurate shading of sound for each vowel, or several shadings all mixed together? Correcting a faulty vowel will often simply allow the richness—that is, the "beauty"—you are seeking to come into the tone.

2. *To produce an accurate vowel color, you have to* think *it precisely*. Remember, your sound-making mechanism carries out the instructions your brain gives it. *Vague concepts produce vague sounds.* In conversation we often speak so quickly that we can ignore small changes of vowel sounds and dropped consonants; since everyone does it, we all understand each other. When we sing the same words, however, we stretch out the mistakes with the tone, and they become so glaring that we cannot ignore them. To correct those mistakes, we must have an accurate concept of both what the vowel or consonant is and how we make it. You may not be aware that your concepts are vague or faulty until you are called on to make slight adjustments in the color of your vowels because people say that they can't understand you or that you are mispronouncing certain words.

3. *Accurate vocal coloring depends on the coordinated operation of the entire phonation machine.* Clear concepts, deep breathing, open throat and jaw, and full resonance must work together by habit to support the correct positions of vowels, if tonal coloring is to be consistent and accurate. It is the working together of the whole system that produces the desired result, not simply the operation of a single part or function. Keep this principle in mind when you become aware of mistakes you are making in vowel color, so that in correcting them you do not actually hamper some other phase of the phonation machine's operation through strain or added tension.

If your choir included the governor of Kansas, the mayors of Boston and Birmingham, a citizen of Stockholm, a Japanese business executive, and a Texas rancher, and the director asked them to sing "AH" together on the same pitch, the result would be six different simultaneous colors of sound. Each person would swear that his or her tone had the "right" quality, because that is what each is used to at home. Yet differences would be obvious, and, if the choir were to achieve a secure blend, each one of the colors would have to be somewhat modified.

Training your voice to make accurate vowel colors starts with becoming aware of the sounds you now are accustomed to making and noting which ones need to be modified in order to give your singing greater consistency and accuracy according to generally accepted standards. This is based on the demonstrable fact that *consistency requires the elimination of undesirable mixtures of color*. In the title of this lesson, the phrase "a Kansas Yankee from Birmingham" represents the attempt to weld together three contrasting accents, or ways of producing vocal colors—midwestern, New England, and southern. Such mixtures are hard to control, in a choir and in your own singing. Rather than trying to build your personal tone control on such combinations, you need to establish in your habits the basic, uniform, widely accepted sound values for each vowel and consonant.

CLASS ACTIVITIES

1. The class will sing Exercises 16.1–16.3 as a group, in smaller groups, and individually. Notice that each exercise focuses on small differences of vowel color or individual vowels with which many singers have trouble. Can you hear the differences when the whole class sings? When other individuals sing? When you sing? Make note of those you have trouble hearing or producing distinctly, and review them after studying Lesson 17. Observe whether you have added difficulty with particular sounds because of high or low notes, weak breath support, or some sort of throat strain.

Exercise 16.1.

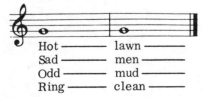

Hot ——— lawn ———
Sad ——— men ———
Odd ——— mud ———
Ring ——— clean ———

Exercise 16.2. Transpose up and down by half steps.

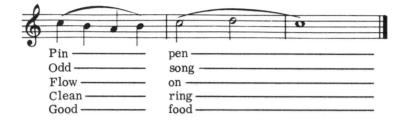

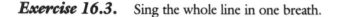

Pin	pen
Odd	song
Flow	on
Clean	ring
Good	food

Exercise 16.3. Sing the whole line in one breath.

OO
OH
Mid
Mad

(Add other vowels as desired.)

2. Sing a familiar song for the class, concentrating on your pronunciation of the word sounds. Record your performance if possible. After the playback have members of the class tell you which vowels they thought were not quite accurate, which consonants they could not hear, and any other faults of coloring the tone that they could detect.

ON YOUR OWN

1. Using an exaggerated southern accent (or other idiom you know), sing a familiar song before your mirror, and watch exactly what you do to make the exaggeration. Which vowels do you change? How? What is the nature of the change? When you isolate the difference, can you control the degree to which you use it?

2. Listen to recorded performances in several styles of music. Try to hear some opera, light opera, oratorio, or sacred music, and popular styles. Do you hear any coloring in the singing that sounds wrong, or affected? Are there differences between serious styles and popular styles? What are they? If you listen to singing in a foreign language, can you hear sounds that are not part of English (such as the German *ö*) that you can imitate?

LESSON 17

Vowels and Diphthongs

CONCEPTS

You expect the American flag to be red, white, and blue. The same design in green, yellow, and purple would look distorted and wrong.

Some singing suffers from a similar distortion when the singer makes vowel colors that aren't accurate. Lesson 16 stressed the importance of controlling vowel color in speaking and singing. In order to make such control possible, we will now examine the specific positions and sounds of the principal vowels of the English language.

We said that accurate vowel color is virtually the same as pure tone quality. Stated another way, accurate vowels equal resonant tone. *Resonant* implies rich, amplified, supported, clear, and projected tone, which are terms that could apply to pure tone also but that explain it in more detail. The statement could also be read the other way around: resonant tone equals accurate vowels. Making a secure, accurate vowel color for the word you are singing helps you to sing a resonant tone; and concentrating on a resonant, deeply supported tone will make it easier for you to sing accurate vowels.

When you speak, you use many shadings of vowel color easily and quickly. You may never have had to determine exactly what you do to make each of those shadings, yet you need just such precise information to achieve pinpoint control of vowel production. To help you organize the vowel sounds you use in singing, we list ten basic vowels, ranging roughly from the "darkest," which you probably feel back in your throat, to the "brightest," which is usually felt toward the front of the mouth. Choosing only ten of the many shadings available might be compared to crossing a stream by stepping on only ten large, secure boulders while avoiding many smaller, less secure rocks lying between. If you feel secure on the boulders, you can step on the smaller stones when you need to.

Ten Basic Vowels

OO as in MOON   AH as in LOT
OO as in FOOT   AH as in MAD
OH as in MOAN   EH as in BED
AW as in LAWN   IH as in BID
UH as in MUD   EE as in ME

Dictionaries use other systems of phonetic symbols to represent these sounds, as well as other vowel shadings that fall between them. The International Phonetic Alphabet (IPA) is one such system that is particularly useful, because it helps you produce sounds in various languages in addition to English. As you go farther with voice training, it will become increasingly important to learn such systems so that you can distinguish more subtle shadings than this list supplies. Private voice training normally goes into more detail about vowel sounds than is possible in a class situation You are encouraged to begin such training as soon as you can, if you intend to reach for real achievement in singing.

The ten basic vowels given here are purposely spelled with symbols you can recognize, for quick reference and easy remembering. When you drill on accurate production of these sounds, use your familiarity with the sounds, as they occur in the sample words, to build accuracy and consistency in your production. Say the vowels. Then sing them. Compare the sound you make in speaking with the one you sing. Learn the exact position, feeling, and sound of each vowel as you produce it. You must realize that this can be done only by physically producing the sound; it cannot be done by merely thinking it. The vowel results from the interaction of your mental concept with the action of your sound-producing mechanism.

It is important that you become aware of the many spellings possible for each vowel sound. For example, the OO sound is used in moon, through, rue, few, rude, who, two, and you, among others. Every vowel can be spelled more than one way, but the difference in spelling does not change the basic sound.

Diphthongs

A diphthong is a *combination vowel*—two vowels sounded in succession in the same syllable, with no consonant between. In English there are at least five diphthongs, and possibly six.

IE	as in LIE or BY	=	<u>AH</u> + (EE)
OY	as in BOY or OIL	=	<u>AW</u> (or <u>OH</u>) + (EE)
OW	as in NOW or PLOUGH	=	<u>AH</u> + (OO)
EW	as in FEW or DUE	=	(EE) + <u>OO</u>
AY	as in MAY or LAID	=	<u>EH</u> + (EE)

Some authorities add OH as a diphthong, as in GROW—<u>OH</u> + (OO). Others say that the AY sound is not a diphthong, but a single vowel color, as in DAY. To some extent such differences of opinion are accounted for by the context of the word in which the sound occurs. For your own security in the production of these sounds, you need to discover which way allows you to make the most exact colors each time you sing them.

The basic rule in singing diphthongs is that the two component vowels are of unequal length. The longer of the two is called the *sustaining vowel,* and in the chart above it is underlined. It ordinarily occupies about nine tenths of the total time of the diphthong. The other component is the *vanishing vowel,* shown above in parentheses, which occupies the remaining tenth of the total time. To illustrate this relationship, the word "my," which includes the diphthong <u>AH</u> + (EE), would be diagrammed as follows:

```
    | – Total Duration of the Diphthong —|
    |—+—+—+—+—+—+—+—+—+—+——|
M – AH _____ (EE)
```

If you do not make this timed relationship perfectly clear as you sing a diphthong, you distort the word badly. To make this obvious, you need only sing the two component vowels for equal lengths of time:

M – <u>AH</u> _____ (EE) _____

Failure to sing both vowels in a diphthong can lead you to sing a different word unintentionally. For example, the word "our" is spelled phonetically:

<u>AH</u> + (OO) + R = OUR

If you don't sing the vanishing vowel (OO) you will sing:

<u>AH</u> + R = ARE

Then there's the word "hail," which is spelled phonetically:

H + <u>EH</u> + (EE) + L = HAIL

Without the vanishing vowel you find yourself singing:

H + EH + L = HELL

Remember that diphthongs, like the vowels that comprise them, can be spelled in different ways. Train yourself to see the *sound* when reading a word, and not to be confused by the spelling. For example, the <u>AH</u> + (EE) diphthong can be spelled pie, fly, buy, sigh, guide, aisle, choir, feist, and aye.

CLASS ACTIVITIES

1. The class will sing Exercise 17.1 all together, in small groups, and individually. Sing all the vowels listed, using the most consistent, accurate, and resonant tone you can produce for each vowel. Observe and remember which vowels were easiest for you and which hardest. In either case, can you discover why?

Exercise 17.1. Vowels.

2. The class will sing Exercise 17.2 as a class, in small groups, and individually. Begin by *thinking* the vowel clearly. Then *speak* it in a full voice, as though to a large audience. Then *sing* the same tone and vowel color, as indicated. If this is recorded, observe on playback whether you change the vowel color between speaking and singing or in singing from the higher note to the lower. Can you discover what you change if this happens?

Exercise 17.2.   Vowel words.

Think: Go	*Say:* GO	*Sing:* GO!___
Soon	SOON	SOON!-__
Put	PUT	PUT!___
Putt	PUTT	PUTT!-__
Law	LAW	LAW!___
Odd	ODD	ODD!___
Sad	SAD	SAD!___
Red	RED	RED!___
Did	DID	DID!___
See	SEE	SEE!___

3.   The class will sing Exercise 17.3 as a class, in small groups, and individually. Use the same procedure as in Exercise 17.2, but carry the sustaining vowel of the diphthong from the higher tone to the lower and put the vanishing vowel on at the end (at the beginning for "Few") so that the relationship between the two vowels sounds accurate—or, more simply, so that the diphthong sounds correct.

Exercise 17.3.   Diphthong words.

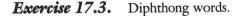

Think: My	*Say:* MY!	*Sing:* MY!_____
Boy	BOY!	BOY!_____
May	MAY!	MAY!_____
Grow	GROW!	GROW!___
Few	FEW!	FEW!_____

(vanishing vowel precedes sustaining vowel)

4.   The class will sing and record Exercise 17.4. Sing all tones in each phrase with uniform vowel color and power, on one breath. Observe closely which vowel colors are easiest and which hardest for you to sing, and try to determine what you are doing in each case. Notice that the exercise uses each of the ten basic vowels at least once.

Exercise 17.4.   Transpose up or down.

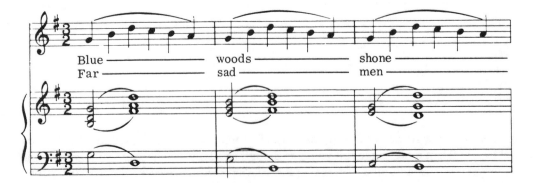

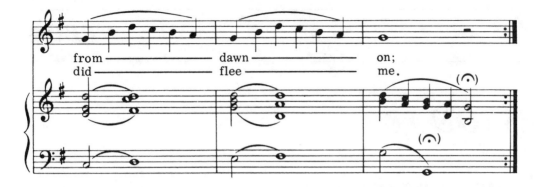

from ——————— dawn ——————— on;
did ——————— flee ——————— me.

5. Copy the following lines on a separate sheet of paper:

a. Few boys now cry as loudly as they like to say they might.

b. Try your new trowel in the brown soil around the roots of a few of these fine bright flowers.

Over each word that contains a diphthong, write out the sustaining vowel (and underline it) and the vanishing vowel (in parentheses). After all the sounds are written, take turns reading the lines to each other aloud, being sure to sound every vowel in the diphthongs in the right proportion. What effect does this have on the clarity of the words?

ON YOUR OWN

1. Go to your mirror. Speak and sing the ten basic vowels in the words given in the list on p. 67. Study the position of your lips, jaw, throat, and tongue as you normally pronounce the words. What happens when you speak and sing them loudly, as if for a large audience? What happens when you whisper them to someone across the room?

2. In the music of a familiar song, write above the words the symbol for every vowel you must sing. How many are among the ten basic vowels? Which ones need some other shading? After you have written the symbols, sing the song, paying special attention to everything you have written. Does this make the words clearer? Your tone better?

3. In the same song, locate and write out the symbols for every diphthong in the words. Remember that each can be spelled in a variety of ways.

LESSON 18

Consonants

CONCEPTS

Consonants are stoppages or interruptions of tone. They shape tone into meaningful units that we recognize as words. If consonants are not clear and understandable, even the richest, most resonant singing tone is limited in meaning. When people tell you, "I can't understand your words," "Your diction is poor," or "You should enunciate more clearly," they are saying that you haven't made clear, precisely articulated consonants. The remedy for this fault is quite simple: You must know what the consonants are and precisely how you produce each one.

As you are acquiring this knowledge it is important to keep in mind that the clearest consonants will result from the precise coordination of tongue, lips, and vocal folds and that they are rarely, if ever, helped by strain, tension, or exaggeration.

Table 18.1 lists the consonants of the English language. Notice that the letter-symbols used represent *sounds you make,* and not merely alphabet letters. Some letters have more than one sound, such as the *c* in "capacity"; others have no single unique sound, such as *q* and *x,* but borrow sounds from other letters, depending on the context of the word in which they appear.

Table 18.1.   Chart of English Consonants.

Voiced Explosives (Pitch Accompanies Stoppage)	How Produced	Unvoiced Explosives (Pitch Follows Stoppage)
Group I. *Explosive Consonants* (made by a sudden release of a complete stoppage of tone or breath)		
B as in BAT ⟶	Lips closed, teeth apart ⟵	P as in PAT
D as in DOG ⟶	Tip of tongue at gum line behind upper front teeth ⟵	T as in TOG
G as in GIVE ⟶	Tongue arched against roof of mouth; compare with NG sound ⟵	K as in KING
J as in JEER ⟶	Teeth almost closed; tongue makes stoppage against front roof of mouth with tip down, behind lower front teeth; compare with ZH-SH ⟵	CH as in CHEER

Group II. *Sustaining Consonants* (made by air escaping through a partial stoppage)

V as in VINE ──────→ Lower lip held loosely against ←────── F as in FINE
upper teeth; air escapes between

Z as in ZEAL ──────→ Tongue arched, with tip down ←────── S as in SEAL
behind lower front teeth; air
escapes between tongue and roof
of mouth

T̲H̲ as in T̲H̲Y ──────→ Tip of tongue out between front ←────── TH as in THIGH
teeth; air escapes around it

ZH as in PLEASURE ──→ Position as for J-CH, but held ←────── SH as in SHOUT
more loosely so that air escapes

L as in LAY ──────→ Tip of tongue touches gum line ←────── No equivalent
behind upper front teeth while
vowel UH is said

M as in MAY ──────→ Lips closed as for B-P; tone is ←────── No equivalent
sustained with air escaping
through nose

N as in NOW ──────→ Tip of tongue in D-T position; ←────── No equivalent
tone is sustained with air escap-
ing through nose

NG as in RING ──────→ Tongue arched as for G-K; tone ←────── No equivalent
is sustained with air escaping
through nose

UR as in PURR ──────→ Tongue cupped with sides touch- ←────── R as in RICH (Short; has
ing upper side teeth   very slight tone value)

Group III. *Aspirates* (breath only; no tone, no stoppage)

No equivalent ──────→ Open, "panting" formation of ←────── H as in HOW
jaw and mouth; sound made by
slight constriction of airstream in
throat

No equivalent ──────→ Blow through mouth position ←────── WH as in WHY
used for blowing out candle

Group IV. *Vowel-formation Consonants* (made by forming to produce a vowel, but not making the tone)

No equivalent   Position to produce OO: W as in WILL
(OO) + IH + L

No equivalent   Position to produce EE: Y as in YET
(EE) + EH + T

In using the chart, focus on the sound itself. Observe the action of your tongue, lips, and jaw as you produce the sound. The consonants are listed in four principal groups, according to how the sound stoppage is made, so it is important that you become aware of exactly what you are doing to articulate each one. In the first two groups, explosive consonants and sustaining consonants, equivalent consonant sounds are listed in pairs in which the stoppage position is virtually the same for both sounds. The difference between the two is found in the fact that in voiced explosives phonation (here called *pitch*) happens at the same time as the stoppage; in unvoiced explosives phonation begins immediately after the stoppage is released. This is a small, but immensely important difference. Over half of all consonant sounds are related to it, and you simply will not be understood if you do not master it.

Singing clean consonants requires techniques that may at first seem contradictory. The sounds must be sharp, precise stoppages, cleanly articulated so that words can be understood, yet they must not hinder the smooth flow of the vocal line. Consider the analogy of a clothesline: It is strong and continuous so that it will hold clothes off the ground; when you put clothespins on it, in a sense you divide its length into smaller units, but you do not really interrupt the flow of the line itself. Similarly, clear consonants depend on secure tone production, just as the clothespins depend on the clothesline to support them. An unstrained, coordinated production of consonant sounds allows them to be heard clearly without disturbing the continuous flow of the melodic line.

CLASS ACTIVITIES

1.   Write the words of a familiar song on a piece of paper. Above each word write the symbol from Table 18.1 for every consonant used. Check these for accuracy by reading the entire song, leaving out all vowels and reading only the symbols you wrote. An interesting variation is to have each person bring a different familiar song to class to read by consonants only. Have the class guess what the song is after hearing only the consonants.

2.   Read a line of the words in a whisper to someone across the room. Do your best to stress the consonant sounds so that the other person understands you. What does this tell you about precision and coordination as opposed to force or exaggeration?

3.   Sing the song you analyzed in Activity 1, making each consonant clear but keeping in mind that the singing line must be smooth and continuous. Record your performance for playback and class critique. Identify the consonants you habitually slight or leave out altogether.

4.   Sing Exercise 18.1, 18.2, or the song *Model of a Modern Major-General*, p. 174 (following the instructions for 18.2), for the class and for recording. Observe the following things about your production of consonant sounds:

   a.   Which consonants are most difficult for you to sing clearly and easily?

   b.   Is your principal difficulty with making beginning consonants, final consonants, or difficult combinations (tongue twisters)?

   c.   Do your listeners actually hear your consonants as clearly as you think you are making them? If not, can you discover specific ways of conveying consonant sounds more clearly while still avoiding strain or exaggeration?

Exercise 18.1.   Sing each nonsense phrase smoothly, without rushing. Articulate each consonant clearly and keep the tone flowing without interruption.

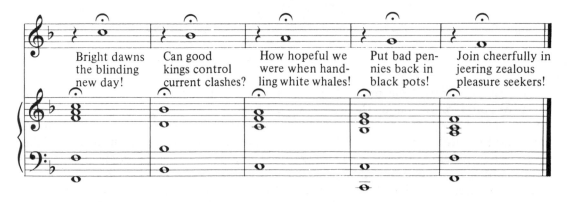

Exercise 18.2.   Learn this exercise thoroughly so that you can sing it as fast as possible and still allow each consonant sound to be heard clearly. Sing in a manner that projects the words to a medium-sized audience.

TRIO

William Gilbert

Arthur Sullivan
From The Mikado

To sit in solemn si-lence in a dull, dark, dock, In a

pe-sti-len-tial prison with a life – long lock, A–wait-ing the sensation of a

short, sharp, shock from a cheap and chippy chopper on a big, black block!

ON YOUR OWN

1. Make a list of the consonant sounds that are most difficult for you to produce clearly. Invent your own tongue twisters using those sounds, and practice saying them rapidly in front of a mirror. Try to find out exactly what gives you the most trouble: not moving your tongue quickly enough, tense jaw muscles, wrong position of the consonant itself, and so on.

To invent your tongue twisters, open a dictionary to the letter giving you the trouble; compose a meaningful sentence from words beginning with that letter. Try to include both *voiced explosives* and *unvoiced explosives* as you make the sentence longer; this means you must look up the letter that stands for the matching sound. For example, if the D-T combination of sounds is the problem, you could build the sentence: "Ted's dad tried dinning tiny, tinny ditties into Ted's tired dome!" Cram as many of the same or related sounds into the line as you can. Include some words that have the sounds in the middle as well as at the beginning or end, for example, "ditties."

2. Using a hand mirror so that you can watch the action closely, review all of the consonant sounds out loud. Observe your physical appearance as you make each one. Spend extra time on those you still consider troublesome. As an experiment, exaggerate some of the sounds by force or strain, noting the extent and nature of the muscle tightening you do to produce them.

LESSON 19

What Is Placement?

CONCEPTS

You may have heard singers talk about *placement* when speaking of the way they make tone. Like many musical terms, it is just vague enough to be confusing unless you understand what it means about the way you make tone yourself.

Obviously, tone is produced in the larynx, so placement in the sense of adjusting the location of tone production is just not possible. However, vowel coloring and resonance *can* be adjusted, so placement makes sense when understood in those terms.

The most direct way to understand placement is by referring to the physical sensations you experience in making various kinds of tones. When you hum, you feel the sensation in your lips and nose. By contrast, you feel the OO vowel in your mouth and throat. When you were asked to sing the "bright" extreme of tone for the tonal continuum in Lesson 12, you made a sound that you felt in your nose, while the "dark" extreme was made by swallowing the tone deep in your throat. All of these changes, or tone-production methods, have something to do with vowel color or resonance, even though your immediate understanding of them springs from the sensations they produce in specific locations.

The objective of placement is to control tone production in a way that equalizes these sensations and smoothes out the vocal line, so that you have the feeling, as you sing, that you are keeping the tone in one place. *Forward placement* is often held up as the ideal. This means a tone production in which the sensations of tone seem to focus under the bridge of the nose, or "in the mask," as it is often described.

Several lessons have pointed out that the best tone results from the coordinated operation of your entire phonation machine: clear mental concepts, correct posture, deep breath support, normal larynx position, open throat and jaw, and full resonance. This applies completely to forward placement, which will happen only when the whole machine works as a unit to produce it. When it does, the vocal apparatus simply "lets the tone through"—right up to the bridge of the nose, where the sensation is felt.

Most singers find that this is easier to do on some vowels than on others. The vowels that seem most clear, accurate, and relaxed in production may in fact feel that way because they already have considerable forward placement. The goal, of course, is to develop one consistent production that will let *every* vowel come through with accurate color, with uniform resonance, and without strain or distortion. When this begins to happen in your singing, you will recognize it, if only because you sing with greater ease and freedom.

Once again, a word of caution: Forward placement is *not* the same as nasal tone—they are exact opposites. You make nasal tone by *preventing* the tone from resonating in the nasal passages. You close off those passages at the back of your throat or by holding your nose, so that the tone sounds pinched and blocked, producing a quality you understand as "nasal." By contrast, forward placement uses all available nasal resonance, adding it to the resonance produced in the throat and mouth.

The exercises of this lesson are designed to help you explore the production of forward placement, contrasting it with other qualities, including nasal tone, so that you begin to understand the concept as a personal physical experience rather than simply as a theoretical description.

CLASS ACTIVITIES

1. The class will sing Exercise 19.1 all together and individually, singing all the vowel sounds given. You will feel the HNG and HM sounds under the bridge of your nose; try to make the subsequent vowel happen in the same place. This will probably be easier on AY and EE than on OH and OO, but sing the whole exercise enough times to feel that you *can* control the placement of all the sounds in a uniform way.

Exercise 19.1. Transpose to different keys for variety.

2. The class will sing Exercise 19.2 all together and individually. As you sing, keep the following objectives in mind:

   a. Make consonant sounds by moving only your tongue or lips, and try *not* to move your jaw.

b.   Feel that the tone stays in one place throughout the entire phrase, no matter which vowel sound you are singing; make each vowel move easily to the next without a major change of position.

c.   Sing without identifiable muscular strain; strive for the physical sensation that the tone results from smooth operation of the whole phonation machine. (Check your posture, breathing, vowel colors, clarity of tone, projection, and resonance.)

Exercise 19.2.   Transpose for variety.

Mee may mah moh moo;   Moo moh mah may mee.
Dee day dah doh doo;   Doo doh dah day dee.
Lee lay lah loh loo;   Loo loh lah lay lee.
Kee kay kah koh koo;   Koo koh kah kay kee.

3.   The class will sing Exercise 19.3 (p. 80) all together and individually. Concentrate on the following things as you are singing:

a.   Breathe deeply at every breathing mark (ɔ) even though you may not be completely out of breath. Sing the exercise slowly enough to make this work easily.

b.   Enunciate each word in all three lines clearly. Articulate the consonants with precision, and be sure the vowel color is exact. Keep the vowel color the same for the duration of the word.

c.   Observe exactly where you have problems of tone placement, such as on high notes, on low notes, at your register break, or on specific vowels. If you identify such problems, look for a solution in such things as improved posture, deeper breathing, more open throat, and better projection. Notice that the exercise includes all ten basic vowel sounds. Are you pronouncing each of them correctly?

Exercise 19.3.

ON YOUR OWN

As you listen to singers on radio or television, focus your attention on their tone quality, trying not to listen to their expression or styling. Classify each voice according to whether you feel it is predominantly "bright" or "dark" in quality. Follow their phrasing and melody lines closely to see if you can identify moments when they run into problems of placement—and what they do about them. Try to identify with what you feel are their best tones, imagining their physical sensations in producing them.

Putting the Parts Together

We have stressed several times that singing is a single, coordinated act. The importance of this may have been overshadowed in the item-by-item analysis we have been doing, but its urgency cannot be overemphasized. All the elements of singing (concepts, posture, breathing, phonation, tone coloring, and resonance) must function simultaneously if singing is to be the result. If the process does not work that way, none of the individual elements has much meaning.

The next step in building your voice is to begin putting together the elements we have been analyzing. Until this "putting together" process happens in a way that allows the elements to be governed by habit rather than by your conscious thought, the interaction between them that produces what you think of as "singing" cannot get started. Since that particular kind of phonation is the foundation on which you build your ability to sing expressively, this is a crucial step on your road to vocal control.

CONTENTS OF STEP 5

Lesson 20   ***Seeing Words as Successions of Sounds***
Recognizing that words are controllable patterns of sound as well as units of meaning; the importance of having all component sounds present in the right order to produce a meaningful singing line.

Lesson 21   ***Legato Technique: The Smooth Vocal Line***
The nature of smooth (connected) singing, and why it is the essential component of singing as contrasted with speaking.

Lesson 22   ***Making Phrases***
Grouping words in a singing line together for meaning; phrasing as an ultimate "putting together."

LESSON 20

Seeing Words as Successions of Sounds

CONCEPTS

When you talk, you speak *meanings*. Because you are thinking about conveying those meanings, you may overlook the fact that the words you are speaking are actually organized patterns of the very sounds we have been dealing with in Step 4.

Since others understand you when you speak, this may seem to be an unimportant technicality. Yet when you sing a continuous melodic line it becomes very important, because the act of sustaining tone through a word changes the normal relationships of the sounds within that word. This sustained tone may reveal that you have left out some sounds, elided them (run them together), or made the wrong sound colors. When you discover such an error, you need to find out what the precise succession of sounds must be to produce the words you are having trouble with; until you can produce such a succession, your singing will not be very understandable.

Our speech habits train us to be careless about making sounds. Most of us speak rapidly, and by common, unspoken agreement we tend to leave out or elide many sounds called for by the words we use. In addition, English contains many silent letters (such as the final *e* in "fine," or the second *t* in "letter") and many combinations of letters that have multiple pronunciations. The OUGH combination is an example. The GH is usually silent, except in "cough" and "rough," for example, where it is pronounced as "F"; the OU has several different pronunciations, each using a different vowel or diphthong color. Here are five:

Though he wore a mask, he coughed as he ploughed through the dusty, rough ground.

  (OH)   (AW)   (OW)   (OO)   (UH)

Since this is a complicated—and not too logical—arrangement, we have learned simply to accept the spelling and *see the words as successions of sounds*. If someone says, "I don't understand what you just said," we try to clarify it by enunciating the sounds themselves more precisely.

Just such precise enunciation is required to make singing lines understandable. The first step in developing pronunciation and enunciation skill is to perceive what sounds are called for in a line and how they are made. Acquiring this skill allows your richest tones to be heard without interference and makes it possible for your singing to convey meaning in a manner similar to speaking clearly. It forces you *not* to mumble, elide, garble, or omit sounds. It allows you to fulfill the demands of the music itself, which assigns to each sound a specific duration value and, by so doing, structures the ingredient of phonation that is not present in speaking: controlled tone and pitch through measured periods of time—in short, a melody line.

If your habits don't as yet let you immediately recognize what sounds *should* be produced in a line of words, you will not make them correctly and will not be understood; any meaning or expression you want to convey in singing the line will not get across. You need to train your mind to recognize at sight the succession of sounds that must be articulated to produce a line of words.

Below are the words of the song *Take My Heart* (p. 232), with their component sounds written out to show how the process works. All of these symbols are taken from Lessons 17 and 18, using only the ten basic vowels (p. 67) even where more subtle shadings might be possible. The succession contains every word sound you would have to sing to make the word complete. Study this example carefully, and use it as a reference for the Class Activities. A useful first step is to cover the actual words and read the sound-symbols aloud, giving each one equal duration and loudness. From this succession of sounds, word patterns will emerge. When this is clear to you, carry the technique over into singing the same words.

Take	my	heart	into	your	care,
T EH(EE) K	M AH(EE)	H AH R T	IH N T OO	(EE) OO UR	K EH UR

and	soothe	its	sorrow	and
AH N D	S OO TH	IH T S	S AH R OH	AH N D

complaining;
K UH M P L EH(EE) N IH NG

Or,	once	again	before	we	part,
AW UR	(OO) UH N S	UH G EH N	B EE F OH R	(OO) EE	P AH R T

Ah!	hold	me	fast!
AH	H OH L D	M EE	F AH S T

My	lips	that	always	met	you
M AH(EE)	L IH P S	TH AH T	AW L (OO) EH(EE) Z	M EH T	(EE) OO

smiling,
S M AH(EE) L IH NG

That	spoke	sweet	words	into	your	ear,
TH AH T	S P OH K	S(OO) EE T	(OO) UR D Z	IH N T OO	(EE) OO UR	IH UR

Smile,	alas,	no	more,	but	are	cursing
S M AH(EE) L	UH L AH S	N OH	M OH UR	B UH T	AH R	K UR S IH NG

Those	who	drove	me	from	you!
TH OH Z	H OO	D R OH V	M EE	F R UH M	(EE) OO.

CLASS ACTIVITIES

1. Using *Take My Heart* or another song that you have analyzed by its component sounds, do the following things in order:

   a. Read the sound-symbols aloud, without thinking of them as words, giving each one equal stress.

   b. Sing the melody in the same manner, taking care *not* to make meaningful words or sing expressively.

   c. Sing the song again, combining the sounds into meaningful words. Use the most "ideal" tone you can command, and be sure your audience understands every word you sing. Notice whether you can sense any relationship between making accurate sounds, conveying meaning, and producing beauty of tone. Hold a class critique for each person who sings.

2. As a written assignment, analyze the words of a song from the Song Collection of this book, using the *Take My Heart* analysis as a model. To make this the most instructive exercise possible, you should do *all* of the following things. *Don't skip any of them.*

   a. Write the words on a separate sheet of paper, leaving a wide space after each word and between each line.

   b. *Read each word out loud before writing its sound-symbols.* This is crucial. Listen to the sounds you make in saying the word out loud, and then find the exact symbols for those sounds.

   c. Write under each word the symbols for the sounds you have made, using *only* the following:

      1. The ten basic vowels of Lesson 17 (p. 67). Don't add others; if you think a sound is slightly different from one of them, use the one you think is closest.

      2. The diphthongs listed in Lesson 17 (p. 68). Write the symbols for both the sustaining and the vanishing vowels, with underlining and parentheses, not simply the single sound-symbol for the diphthong.

      3. The consonants of Lesson 18 (p. 72). Be sure you have all the necessary underlining and parentheses correctly written.

   d. Cover the words and read aloud the sound-symbols you have written. If you read exactly what you wrote, any errors will be immediately obvious to your ear.

3. Come to class prepared to write on the blackboard a line of word sounds representing a familiar song you have chosen; do not write the actual words or tell the class that song it is. The class members can then compete to see who can identify the song first by reading the sounds to themselves. Write the songs out in the following manner:

G AH D B L EH S UH M EH R IH K UH L A͡H N D T͡H A͡H
T A͡H(EE) L UH V.

SH O͡O D OH L D U͡H K (OO) E͡H(EE) N T UH N S B EE
F OH R G AH T A͡H N D N EH V UR B R AW T T OO
M A͡H(EE) N D.

4. Using a different song (familiar or new), sing the words without previously writing out the component sounds. As you sing, try to see each sound in the word as you did in Activity 1; try to make your performance convey the word meaning clearly, too. Can you develop a habit of instant analysis?

ON YOUR OWN

Listen closely to recordings of singers performing in English, and watch singers on television. Remember to listen to both serious (religious, operatic, concert) and popular styles. As you observe and compare, try to determine:

1. Why can some singers be understood better than others?

2. With which sounds do they seem to take special care?

3. Do their consonants interfere with a smooth, flowing line of tone? If their words are understandable, does their consonant production sound artificial or natural?

4. Does the accuracy of their vowel colors correspond with the pleasing quality of their tone?

LESSON 21

Legato Technique: The Smooth Vocal Line

CONCEPTS

Which of these diagrams best represents the way you sing a melody line?

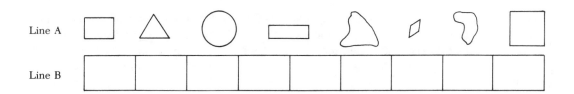

Line A

Line B

If you run out of breath, have trouble with high or low notes, find some vowels hard to sing resonantly, are troubled by register breaks, have difficulty making clear consonants, or strain muscles in any way, your singing is probably best represented by Line A, in which tones are uneven in size, uncertain in shape, and separated by gaps.

Line B, by contrast, represents the secure tonal production needed for expressive singing—the *continuous vocal line*. This has been called *legato technique*, and it is based on the Italian term *legato*, meaning "connected." As Line B suggests, this kind of singing carries one tone on to the next with equal power and size, no breaks in tone production, and no distorted vowels, exaggerated consonants, or overaccented tones.

Like other aspects of successful singing, legato technique combines several accomplishments. When all of these operate together as a result of habit, you are able to sing a tonal line that can be expressively shaped. These accomplishments are, of course, the very techniques we have been dealing with in previous lessons. The product of their working together is a smooth, flowing vocal line, which is the next major step on your road to expressive singing. Here are the basic requirements for singing such a smooth line.

Four Fundamentals of Legato Technique

1. *Habitually correct posture and diaphragmatic-costal breathing.* Not only are the breathing techniques discussed in Lesson 8 still important but they must also have become unshakable habits from which your singing springs, if you are to accomplish real legato technique.

2. *Controlled, accurate vowel colors.* Your production of vocal colors must be precise, complete, and not blurred. Vowel placement must be accurate and supported by open, strain-free tone production. You will probably find that singing a legato line becomes an easy and natural next step when such tone production has become habitual.

3. *Precise, unforced articulation of consonants.* All consonant stoppages should be clearly recognizable and heard as part of the smooth vocal line rather than as obstructions to its flow.

4. *An even scale.* Your entire singing range, from lowest to highest tone, should develop one basically uniform quality. This results from achieving control over the natural changes of production such as register breaks, differences between "bright" and "dark" vowel placements, and changes of dynamics. The even scale results from putting together such vocal techniques as open, resonant phonation, effortless control of register changes, accurate vowel colors, and (of course) deep breath support.

The diagrams at the beginning of this lesson are useful images to keep in mind while you are singing, as well as when you listen to others. When you are hearing fine artists in person or on recordings, notice how much of their singing corresponds to the concept of Line B and how much of their effectiveness seems to result from their ability to sing a smooth vocal line. In your own singing, try to reproduce in tone your mental concept of Line B and avoid that of Line A. If you do this consistently, it will progressively strengthen your best habits of tone production.

CLASS ACTIVITIES

1. The class will sing Exercises 21.1 and 21.2 all together and then individually. The first time through, consciously sing the melody in the style of Line A, exaggerating differences between tones and the gaps between them. The second time, sing in the manner suggested by Line B, stressing the smooth continuity and even quality of the tones. In each case, observe what you do specifically to make your voice produce the particular line you are singing. Are you able to feel physically the control you need to produce an effective Line B? What specific problems hinder you from singing a smooth line all the way to the end? In Exercise 21.2, can you sing high and low tones, and tones on each end of large intervals such as the octave, with uniform placement and breath support?

2. Record Exercises 21.1 and 21.2. As you sing, consciously try to produce your most consistent ideal tone, especially relating it to your effort to sing in the style of Line B. When hearing the playback, evaluate what you hear in the following ways, and have others in the class contribute reactions:

   a. Does your ideal tone help you produce a smoother vocal line?

   b. What specific faults interfered with your singing either your ideal tone or a smooth line? Running out of breath? Faulty vowel placement? Uncontrolled register changes? Muffled consonants? Fear of high notes?

   c. If you hear that you have sung notes of a Line A type, can you sing them again in the Line B manner, within the vocal line that gave you trouble the first time? What must you do to change them? Try to discover specific corrections for specific faults.

Exercise 21.1. Slowly. Use all breathing marks.

AH_____ OH_____ AW_____
EE_____ OO_____ AY_____

Exercise 21.2.

Come a - way! Let — us be go - ing,

Do not stay! Sun - light is glow - ing!

3.   Apply the evaluation process of Activity 2 to your performance of a song being used for class work or prepared for recital. Concentrate on singing each phrase or line of words in a pure legato style from first note to last. Observe whether being able to do so helps you to convey the meaning of the song to your audience.

ON YOUR OWN

1. Sing a familiar song before your mirror, consciously giving your tonal line three shapes in succession:

   a. The shape of Line B.

   b. The shape of Line A. Make each tone equal in quality and loudness.

   c. A shape with all the expression you feel should be put into an ideal performance.

Exaggerate each performance; ham it up. When you have heard yourself sing all three completely, reevaluate your concept of *ideal*. Did it resemble Line A or Line B most? How did adding "expression" change the sound of the song or the way you went about singing? Can you isolate specific things you did differently? Do the values of a continuous tonal line and an even scale make themselves evident?

2. Listen to recordings of singers suggested by the instructor, or of those you know to be leaders in the concert and operatic fields. Evaluate their control of legato technique along the same lines used in class critiques. Try to hear more than one, for comparison. Particularly listen to singers recommended by the instructor for their outstanding legato.

LESSON 22

Making Phrases

CONCEPTS

What a difference a little phrasing makes! Observe:

The teacher said the student is stupid.

or

"The teacher," said the student, "is stupid."

Punctuation? Yes. Inflection? Well, yes. What makes the difference, though, is *phrasing*—the way words and ideas are grouped and stressed. The reason behind it all is *meaning*—what is to be said, and how words will be arranged to say exactly that, instead of something else.

By developing a dependable legato technique, you open the way for your first major step toward expressive singing, which is the ability to control phrasing as you sing. This is more complicated than the spoken phrasing illustrated above, but it is an absolutely essential ingredient of any singing that is to convey meaning. The dictionary defines a *phrase* as "a short musical thought" and "a group of related words that form a sense unit expressing a thought." Both definitions stress the element of thought, or meaning, as the distinctive characteristic of phrasing.

At this point in your voice training, you may feel that a musical phrase tends to be a line of music you have trouble singing all the way through without running out of breath. You are quite aware that you shouldn't be breathing in the middle of the line, but when your breath runs out you have little choice. Your first reaction may be that you need to take in more air, but as we pointed out in Lesson 9 the real problem may be that you are letting too much air *out*. What you do with the air is just as important as how much you take in.

Why don't you run out of breath when you talk normally? One reason is that you speak words faster than you sing them. Another is that you don't have to make sustained tone on pitch when you talk. Probably the most basic reason, however, is that when you speak you are trying to *say* something, to communicate ideas or meanings. This causes your phonation machine to group words automatically in ways that convey those meanings, or to *phrase* them. Without your having to think about it, this grouping process assures that you will have enough air to speak all the way through the meaning you want to communicate.

A similar process can control phrasing when you sing. You need to think of a succession of notes and words—the melody—as *a unified meaning that you say by singing*. In contrast to speaking, which uses only word meanings, singing requires two kinds of meanings to be conveyed simultaneously: the meaning of the words and the musical meaning of the melody line. The most singable melodies have a close relationship between word meaning and musical meaning, so they fall easily into natural, understandable phrases.

When learning a song, you should study both the word phrasing and the musical phrasing to be sure of the exact meanings you want to convey. This is the kind of study you used when you read the sentences at the beginning of this lesson. You saw what the meanings were for each grouping of words, and then you read the sentences in ways that made those meanings clear. You need to do this for singing also; it makes no more sense to breathe and thus break up a thought you are expressing with singing than it does to breathe and thus break up a thought you are speaking. If you breathe at the wrong moment, then the continuity of the idea is broken in either case. Thinking about phrasing in this manner may help you overcome the nervous habit of running out of breath in the middle of lines, which makes it hard to sing meaningful phrases.

Here are two suggestions to help you start developing secure habits of phrasing:

1. *Decide what you are trying to say.* What do those phrases *mean*? Remember, meaning is to some extent what you, the singer, understand it to be. If you ignore this, singing is likely to become simply a mechanical reproduction of notes with very little meaning. It would be like speaking in a monotone, which makes meaning hard to understand; you add inflections and tonal shadings precisely because you want spoken words to have specific meanings. Singing is different only because the melody line has a predetermined up and down pattern; you still must add tone qualities, dynamic shadings, and other vocal inflections to give the melody meaning.

2. *Phrase to make sense, and breathe to convey that sense.* You don't run out of breath when you speak primarily because you are trying to convey meaning—or make sense. Similar controls will work in singing. Singing expressively is just one more kind of "sense" you want your singing to display, and when you concentrate on conveying that meaning your phonation machine will automatically provide needed breath support. In addition, this ensures that the meaning you sing will be new and fresh each time you sing; it is a specific form of sense that you are conveying *now*, so it cannot be stereotyped. It is something like kissing: If you *mean* it, you don't kiss in a stereotyped way; on the contrary, you put new meaning into it every time, so it is enjoyable. When you phrase to make sense in singing, that's exactly what you have to do.

CLASS ACTIVITIES

1. Sing Exercise 22.1 twice. The first time, stop at the end of the third measure, and do not sing the final tone. Why does the musical phrase seem unfinished? Can you hear why the melodic, harmonic, and rhythmic patterns all seem incomplete, even though there are no words? Now sing the phrase again, adding the final tone. Notice how adding the expected note at the end completes the "thought" of the phrase in all three patterns. If you took a breath right before the final tone, you would change the meaning of the phrase in a way similar to the change in the sentences at the beginning of this lesson. Try it.

Exercise 22.1.

2. Exercise 22.2 is the first line of the song *America,* with a slight change in the last note. Words have been left out to illustrate the strength of your concept of the melody without them. Sing the melody as written, and notice what a sharp change the final note makes in your concept of the whole line, in spite of the absence of words. This demonstrates that, when you sing a song, errors in melodic tones do just as much damage to the meaning of the melody as wrong words do to the meaning of the text. To confirm this, sing the melody correctly with the words (the song is on p. 255), and notice how securely you phrase it, principally because both word and musical meanings are correct.

Exercise 22.2.

3. Using *Drink to Me Only with Thine Eyes* (p. 270), *Litany* (p. 210), or another song chosen by the instructor, prepare and demonstrate to the class the following techniques of word phrasing:

a. Read the first phrase of the song aloud in a full, resonant tone, as though addressing a large audience. Then immediately tell the listeners, in different words, what the phrase *says.* Some examples:

First phrase: Drink to me only with thine eyes, and I will pledge with mine;
Different words: Don't drink a toast to me with wine; let your eyes show that you care as much as I do.

First phrase: Lord, with thankful heart I praise Thee!
Different words: For the blessings I enjoy, I honor and thank you, God.

b. Sing the same phrase to the class, using the original words. Try to convey with your singing the meaning you told the class about in other words.

c. Finish the song in the same manner, phrase by phrase. If you run out of breath during a phrase, try it again, concentrating even more on projecting the meaning. Be sure that you breathe in a deep, diaphragmatic-costal manner.

d. Sing the whole song, as in a recital. Endeavor to convey a continuous flow of meaning, breathing only where the meaning makes it logical to do so. Does your audience listen more closely because you are giving them phrase meanings they can follow?

4. Read the following couplet aloud several times:

I fear my Love may kiss and tell;
My best defense? I'll kiss her well!

Each time you read it, stress a different word. To make this clear, imagine that you are contradicting someone who has just stated it another way. For example, the other person says to you, "You fear your Mother may kiss and tell?" You say (perhaps in amazement), "No, I fear my *Love* may kiss and tell." Or they say, "You fear your Love *will* kiss and tell?" You reply, "No, I fear my Love *may* kiss and tell." Observe that stressing virtually any word in the line gives a new shape and meaning to the whole couplet. How many different meanings can you discover? This couplet is set to music in Lesson 31 (p. 126) if you wish to carry over into singing some of the shadings of meaning you have been speaking here.

5.   Apply the techniques of Activity 3 to a song you are preparing for class performance, particularly if you have encountered trouble with running out of breath in midphrase.

ON YOUR OWN

1.   Read the words of a song you are working on to someone not in this class. Then translate the meaning of the words into your own terms. Even if the original words are rather straightforward in meaning, say the meaning in another way. Try to use your day-to-day manner of speaking. Ask your friend to assist you critically in discovering every possible shade of meaning the words might have.

2.   If a tape recorder or cassette is available to you, record one of your songs in the most meaningful way you can. On playback, pretend that you are a judge of a singing contest in which the recording is one entry. Rate the performance on phrasing, understandability, legato technique, meaning, and expressiveness.

Learning to Perform

When the process of assembling the component parts of singing begins to produce desired results, you need to give attention to the fact that singing is usually done as a means of communicating with other people. This introduces a new element into the single-unified-act nature of singing: It becomes a single-unified-act-while-others-are-watching activity, which automatically injects the element of communication. The simple fact that people are listening introduces an interaction with them that affects the way you sing. Learning to use this to advantage is the bridge to all the realms of singing in which communication is the fundamental premise: expression, interpretation, and conveying meaning and mood.

CONTENTS OF STEP 6

Lesson 23   *Understanding Your Singing as "Performing"*
Understanding what "performance" is, what it requires, and how it affects you while you are singing.

Lesson 24   *Evaluating Your Own Performance*
Use of self-evaluation as a means of improving your control of performance techniques; objective self-analysis as a means of improving vocal and musical performance.

Lesson 25   *Controlling Specific Vocal Faults*
An examination of specific vocal problems that may be intensified by the pressures of performance, with suggested means of controlling them.

LESSON 23

Understanding Your Singing as "Performing"

CONCEPTS

Do you feel that you sing better in the shower than in class? More confidently? With better tone, deeper breathing, and richer resonance? Does everything seem to work well when you are by yourself and then desert you in front of the group?

That's a very common reaction. Self-consciousness undoubtedly accounts for much of it, but other things are also involved. Singing for others introduces a new dimension to vocal production that must be added to those you use in singing only for yourself. This new element can be summed up in the fact that when you sing for others you are *performing*—an activity that moves the whole singing process into a new perspective.

When others are listening, you are aware of your need to communicate something to them with your singing. That, after all, is why you and they are in a performer-audience relationship. Your singing becomes a medium of communication, which takes it well beyond the requirements of simple phonation. Your role as a performer obliges you to convey meaning, give pleasure, express emotion, display technique, entertain, and so on. A whole array of demands is suddenly presented to your subconscious mind as you start. Little wonder if you feel self-conscious or nervous!

The new dimension of vocal production involved in performing is the fact that you must deal with audience reactions as you sing. How do those reactions affect how you breathe, project, phrase, and so on? Performing is a two-way communication. What you are conveying to the audience goes one way, but in return the listeners give back to you a continuous flow of responses *that affect what you do.* They may show that they understand, enjoy, and accept what you are doing, or, on the contrary, they may appear bored, uninterested, and restless. Subconsciously you receive those messages and modify what you are doing according to their nature and intensity. Your level of self-consciousness or confidence, and as a result the whole phonation process, can be materially affected.

Realizing this may make you more nervous about performing, for a while. Such tensions can be controlled by recognizing that the pressures of audience response can be turned to your advantage. Those pressures can make you work harder to control whatever is causing a negative response from your listeners, such as your poor diction, faulty tone, vague meaning, awkward phrasing, or some other specific vocal problem. And, if your audience seems enthusiastic about your performance, that very approval spurs you on to an even more expressive and vital way of singing.

You already react this way in conversation. If you sense that you are getting a negative response to what you are saying, you subconsciously try to change your speaking in some way that will bring a more positive reaction. When the others are clearly "with" you from the outset, chances are that everyone's talking will become more animated and expressive. In either case, your vocal production is modified according to the nature of the two-way communication going on. A similar responsive communication takes place between you and your listeners when you perform successfully.

Here are some recognizable characteristics of successful performing, which are useful in measuring your own performance capabilities. Notice that they deal with mental concepts about singing. Lesson 4, you will recall, pointed out that your singing starts in just such concepts. Every new dimension you add to the singing process must originate in a clear concept of precisely what is involved. Nowhere is this more completely true than in understanding performing.

Four Characteristics of Successful Performing

1. *Your intense motivation is obvious.* Your initial desire to sing has been refined and channeled by the skills you have learned. Now it is demonstrated as an evident desire to sing for others. Your original "want to" now shines forth in your singing as "like to." Performing is not considered a mere assignment, or something you have to do. Instead, you now not only want to *sing* but also want to sing for *others*.

2. *You show confidence in your technical skills.* All the nitty-gritty of voice training—posture, breathing, tone quality, vowel colors, resonance, phrasing, and so on—now works as you sing. The fact that these components do work allows your singing to communicate expressively. If any techniques are still weak or uncertain, performance will reveal specific needs you can strive to fill.

3. *You show that you are challenged, rather than threatened, by pressure.* It is obvious that you love to perform and derive real enjoyment from the interplay between yourself and the audience. The way you sing demonstrates to your listeners that you understand the new dimension of vocal production involved in singing for them and that you are stimulated by it. Above all, you do not appear to be uptight, nervous, or afraid of them.

4. *You show clear understanding of what you want your singing to communicate.* Your audience can discern that you have chosen specific, attractive meanings in the music that you want them to understand. Word meanings, musical meanings, and expression are all accurate and clear; they make sense and probably convey beauty. Your personal problems are not allowed to stand in the way of what you are trying to say as a singer.

If your singing already had all of these characteristics, you would be recognized as a confident, seasoned performer. At your present stage of vocal development, they are most useful as goals that will lead you to the next productive steps of training. In these steps you will be developing the habit of analyzing your performance objectively, as one of your most effective means of improving it; learning to correct specific vocal faults you may encounter during performance; mastering the musicianship needed for expressive singing; and working toward eventual attainment of stage presence.

CLASS ACTIVITIES

1. Each class member will recite the alphabet *as a performance*. As you speak, try to infuse the letters with meanings that *sound* specific. Control your tone, phrasing, emphasis, and mood in ways that will catch the attention of your listeners, even though no actual word meanings are

being spoken. The objective is to make your audience listen to meanings you create with the tone itself. You should discover that the possibilities are almost infinite, and that no two persons will speak the same "meanings." Here is an example: "A! B C D, E F *G*, H I J K L M *N*? O! P Q, R S, T U *V* W. X Y. Z?"

2.   Learn Exercise 23.1 or 23.2 thoroughly, and sing it for the class. This transfers the demands of Activity 1 to a singing line. There are no real words, and the melody line is unfamiliar, even though it may have a musical style that suggests some meaning to you. Try to sing it in a way that communicates to your audience any meanings you do understand or can put into the melody. Tone qualities, rhythms, tempo, vowel colors, and even some suggestions of mood should provide many "meanings" to sing. Remember, such meanings are the substance of your performance for this activity. Can you make your audience pay attention to them and show you by their responses that they understand? (Optional alternative nonsense words have been added.)

Exercise 23.1.

Exercise 23.2.

Bee doo bee doo bee dah dah— Shuh lay lee loh bee doh doh—

Oh bee dah bee dah dah— Shuh lay lee loh bee doh doh!—

3. "Perform" a song you know well and have prepared for class use. Try to make your performance exhibit the four characteristics of successful performance listed in this lesson. Hold class critiques of individual performances to compare reactions about the following:

a. Did the performer seem to be singing because she or he wanted to or because the performance was assigned? What symptoms of either condition were apparent?

b. What technical aspects of the performance went well, and what went poorly? Pay attention to such specifics as posture, breathing, tone, vowel colors, resonance, legato technique, and phrasing.

c. Did the performer sing directly *to* the audience? Was there real two-way communication typical of a successful performance?

4. Attend a live concert of singing, preferably of serious music styles. Observe the performers in terms of the listed performance characteristics. Report to the class, either verbally or in writing, about the following matters:

a. How did the performers show that they wanted to sing? What signs of intense motivation were evident?

b. Which of the performers' technical skills impressed you most? Be as specific as you can.

c. Did the performers seem nervous or afraid of the audience, or poised and in command? In either case, how did they show it?

d. Did they convey clear meanings to *you personally*? What were they? Again, be specific; cite exact things they did or did not communicate.

ON YOUR OWN

1. Sing Class Activity 3 again before your mirror. Compare what you see and hear with your experiences in singing for the class. Does being by yourself still make your performance seem more confident? By some chance, does the lack of an audience make your performance seem mechanical and unrealistic?

2. If facilities for closed-circuit television taping are available, sing Class Activity 2 for videotape playback. Watch yourself as though you were another member of the class, objectively assessing strengths and weaknesses.

LESSON 24

Evaluating Your Own Performance

CONCEPTS

We all like to know "how we did" when we sing for others. What did our listeners hear? What went well? Not so well? Was the meaning we were trying to convey actually understood by the audience? If not, what meaning did they understand?

It isn't easy to evaluate a performance meaningfully. Such words as "good," "wonderful," "poor," or "bad" really don't say much about the specific components that make up a performance, and they are of little help when you want an evaluation that tells you specific things to *do*. More exact language and inclusive analysis are needed.

Since you don't hear yourself the way others hear you, as you discovered when your singing was recorded, self-evaluation is doubly difficult. You rely on the evaluations of others for understanding "how you did," since an important part of what you are "doing" in performance is communicating with them, as Lesson 23 pointed out. When these reactions are given by persons especially qualified by knowledge and experience, such as your instructor, your private voice teacher, or established singers, they can be valuable guides to further development and progress.

Yet it is still *your* voice. Evaluations you make, taking into account all of the information you can obtain, are still the decisive ones—simply because you are the only person in a position to make effective changes in how you sing. This means that the more accurately you evaluate and assess what you are doing, the more immediately you can make those changes. Seen in this way, objective self-evaluation is clearly one of the most effective means of improving your singing performance.

Such accurate self-evaluation calls for the habits of self-discipline discussed in Lesson 5, precisely because you *are* the only one in a position to make evaluations affect what you do. Others may help with suggestions and encouragement, but only you can discipline yourself—and your phonation machine—to actually do what needs doing. Here are some techniques based on self-discipline that have proven effective means of evaluating personal performance:

1. *Listen closely.* Do you actually hear what happens when you sing? Do you focus your full attention on the sounds you make? Do you observe anything beyond the most obvious features (usually something about how nervous you are)? Can you hear small differences in tone quality, the feeling of specific vowel colors, how you control precise consonants, phrasing, and so on?

2. *Be objective.* Do you hear what you are really doing or what you *hope* you are doing? Can you judge your singing without excessive emotion or prejudice, as though, for example, you were in the audience listening to yourself?

3. *Compare.* How did this performance compare with others you have done? With those of other class members or professional singers? Can you make such comparisons in specific terms, avoiding such vague words as *good* and *bad*?

4. *Remember.* What specific things did you set out to do in this performance? Did you accomplish them? If some part of the singing process is not yet working by habit, did you think about it before you started to sing or only after it failed? Can you remember individual tones and phrases that have gone well for you in past performances and what you did to make them work? Can you duplicate them?

Components of a Singing Performance

An effective evaluation must be inclusive, taking account of all the components of your singing performance. It is now time to compile a list of the ingredients of your performance that your audience may be evaluating, consciously or unconsciously, as you perform. This means that you must be aware of them, and the act of recognizing how many different actions and skills are involved may save you from making glaring mistakes through ignorance. Some of these have been discussed in previous lessons; others will be covered later in this book. All of them are important. When we stressed in earlier lessons that singing happens all at once, this list was really what we meant, for these components are the things that "happen" when you sing. Like the numerous parts of your automobile that need to function well to give you a smooth ride, these components must work together efficiently to make a smooth performance.

Vocal Components

1. *Breath Control.* Do habits of correct posture and diaphragmatic-costal breathing support everything you do? Are they really habitual, or do you still have to work at them in ways that are obvious to your audience?

2. *Tone Quality.* What is the actual nature of the singing sounds you make? Clear, focused, natural, expressive, resonant, and controlled? Or strained, breathy, pinched, unsupported, and harsh? Or some mixture?

3. *Accuracy of Vowels and Diphthongs.* Are your vowel colors accurate? Do you sing natural sounds similar to those you speak? Are all your vowels resonant?

4. *Consonants.* Are stoppages precise, clear, and cleanly articulated? Do they interrupt or fit in with the smooth flow of the melody line? Can they be understood?

5. *Legato Technique.* Do you sing a continuous, connected melody line? Does your breathing give it adequate support, so that it sounds easy, or must you work to make it happen? Is it secure enough to permit meaningful phrasing?

6. *Control of Specific Vocal Problems.* Is your vocal technique so secure that you eliminate breathy tones, nasal qualities, harsh or throaty tones, and strained, rigid jaw and throat positions? Do such faults creep in at times without your being able to control them?

Musical Components

1. *Rhythmic Accuracy.* Does your singing display a disciplined rhythmic sense? Does it show that you understand the relations among rhythm, meter, and tempo? Can you read and use rhythmic notation? Does your singing show that you feel rhythm deeply or that you are always a little uncertain?

2. *Acuity of Pitch and Interval.* Do you sing completely accurate pitches? Is your ear sensitive enough to small differences of pitch so that your voice can control them? Does your singing show that you know interval sizes, are familiar with scale patterns, and have an accurate sense of tonality?

3. *Competence in Using the Musical Score.* Does your singing show that you can fluently use staffs, clefs, keys, dynamic markings, phrase markings, and expressive markings? Can you coordinate with an accompanist? How many notational signs does your singing leave out, simply because you don't know their meaning?

4. *Conveyance of Musical Meaning.* Do you sing in a way that communicates both the meaning of the words and their relationship to the musical meaning of what you sing? To what extent must you rely on extramusical meanings (gestures, body movement, exaggerated dynamics, or pseudomusical "expressiveness" such as sliding pitches, sentimental tone quality, or broken rhythms) to give understandable meaning to your singing? Are these added to draw attention from the sounds you make because they are so weak or faulty?

Personal Components

1. *Poise and Mannerisms.* Do you get in the way of your singing? Does your behavior or appearance conflict with the meanings you are singing? Does your singing reflect poise—purposeful self-awareness and control—or only nervous self-consciousness?

2. *Personal Involvement.* Does your singing reflect *you*—your way of phrasing, expressing, or communicating? Does it show that you can convey your own ideas, moods, and nuances, or does it seem to be only a mechanical stringing together of more-or-less musical sounds, learned by imitation of someone else?

CLASS ACTIVITIES

As a class or individual project, work out a usable evaluation sheet for judging all classroom performances from now on. Base it on the performance components discussed above, adding others that may apply to this class situation. To be most effective, the sheet should list in some detail the specific aspects of performance that are to be evaluated and present some explicit, meaningful scale (letter grades, numbers, explanatory comments) with which to rate progress. When the evaluation sheet has been agreed upon by the entire class, it can be used to:

1. Have each class member rate the performance of every singer at class recitals or on testing days; the singer should then be shown all the evaluation sheets as reflections of his or her impact on the audience.

2. Provide the instructor with a uniform means of grading progress and arriving at final grades for the class.

3. Serve as a format for written reports about live concerts attended by class members.

4. Study and analyze the performance techniques of famous singers whose performances can be heard in person, on television, on radio, or on recordings.

Everyone in the class should understand that the objective of this project is to sharpen individual listening habits, so that evaluations will be based on the most intensive perception. The actual rating or evaluation given is much less important than leading the listener to hear and understand better. Consult Appendix 2, p. 147, for a sample evaluation sheet that has proven workable in classroom use.

ON YOUR OWN

When the class evaluation sheet has been developed, ask a few friends not in this class to sit still long enough to hear you sing a song and use the sheet to evaluate your performance. Reflect on the following:

1. Which components on the sheet do they apparently not understand or have questions about? Can you explain these in terms that they do comprehend? What does your explanation reveal about your grasp of the subject?

2. Which components do they understand and respond to immediately? What does this response suggest about the communicative potential of each of the components being evaluated? Are some too specialized to be generally meaningful?

3. Do they comment on matters evidently not included on the evaluation sheet? Are these things important? Should the sheet have covered them?

4. How do their comments compare with those of other class members and your own assessment of your performance? What perspectives on your singing can you gain from the reactions of such laypeople?

LESSON 25

Controlling Specific Vocal Faults

CONCEPTS

When you get sick enough, you go to a doctor to find out what is wrong. The more you hurt, the less you are satisfied with the explanation that you just don't feel well. You want to know exactly what the problem is and what can be done about it. When you realize that it isn't going away—in spite of all the "remedies" you have tried, or because you just ignored it—it's time to get the facts and some help.

Certain persistent singing problems may need to be treated in the same way. You may know that you are doing something wrong, that you are not making headway in solving a problem, but you are still a little hazy about what to do next. You've tried all the cures you know—perhaps including pretending to ignore it—but the fault still gives you trouble. You need specific things to *do*.

This lesson examines four problems that often afflict beginners' singing. For each one we will identify the fault, state some probable causes, describe some of its side effects, and give specific suggestions for correcting it. These are not instant cures. As we have often said, your singing is largely controlled by habit; if a fault is deeply ingrained in your habits, it will take time to replace it with more productive habits. The objective here is to help you bring the problem into clearer focus, so that you will see what has to be changed.

Breathy Tone

What it is	Tone in which the sound of escaping air is audible.
Probable causes	A faulty concept of what a clear tone sounds like.
	Poor posture; weak, shallow breath support.
	Tension of the throat or jaw, which causes faulty adjustment of the vocal folds.
	Distorted, unresonant vowel production.
Side effects	Weak, fuzzy tone quality; little, if any, projection.
	Frequent running out of breath.
	Difficulty in singing complete phrases.
	Limited ability to color tone expressively.

Things to do	To isolate what you do that causes breathiness, do the following:

1. Sing a tone that is *more* breathy than usual.
2. Sing a tone that is *less* breathy than usual, by doing the opposite of what you did in 1.
3. Compare the two tones: What did you change? What *felt* different? Check your posture, depth of breathing, throat tension, vowel placement, and position of your jaw and throat, for possible clues.
4. When you succeed in making a less breathy tone, immediately repeat it several times to begin establishing a new habit.
5. Sing a familiar song, consciously using the less breathy tone production.

Nasal Tone

What it is A twangy tone, which sounds as though you held your nose while singing.

Probable causes Elimination of nasal resonance for one or more of the following reasons:

1. The soft palate or back of the tongue is rising to close off the entrance to the nasal cavities.
2. Your throat or jaw is tense.
3. Weak breath support causes the larynx, throat, and tongue to function in strained positions.

Side effects A piercing, hard quality in all tones.

Badly distorted, flattened vowel colors.

No real resonance to any tone.

What to do To identify the specific feeling of the stoppage that produces the nasal sound, do the following:

1. Hold your nose and sing the most completely nasal sound you can make. Compare this with your normal tone, made without holding your nose. Does your tone have any nasal feeling?
2. Yawn and sing AH, as in Lesson 11. In that position, can you make a tone that has *no* nasal feeling? Hold your nose and sing the yawn-AH tone again; can you make a tone with no nasal feeling that way too? Try to identify what you change in your normal tone production to make the nasal tone happen.
3. Record a familiar song, and check the playback for nasal tones. If you hear any, immediately *reproduce the sound you hear* and then its direct opposite—that is, a tone with all nasal sensation removed. What do you change?
4. Record the song as if it were a performance, using your best legato technique. Try to avoid making nasal tones, but observe where in the song you have the greatest tendency to sing them. Particular vowels? High notes?

Throaty Tone

What it is Tone that sounds caught in the throat, like gargling; tone that has a hard, raspy quality.

Probable causes Severe tension in throat and jaw.

Tone produced in a position similar to swallowing.

Shallow breath support, controlled by "pinching the neck."

Side effects Lack of forward placement, giving all vowels a strained, unnatural sound.

Throat irritation and fatigue, causing "frogs" and the constant need to clear the throat.

A uniformly unpleasant sound that eliminates the possibility of expressive singing.

What to do

1. Record Exercise 17.1 (p. 69). On the playback, identify any vowels that have a throaty sound; then sing the whole exercise using only those vowels, and sing what you feel is a "soft" or "mellow" tone quality, one that is open and relaxed. Compare the feeling of that tone with the tone you made originally, and try to identify the specific changes you make.

2. Sing a familiar song, recording it if possible, in a mood you would describe as "tender," "gentle," or "sweet"—a style in which anything harsh or forceful would be badly out of place. Compare this tone with that you originally made; what feels different?

Closed-Jaw Tone

What it is   Tone forced through a closed mouth, clenched teeth, or a rigid, tight jaw.

Probable causes   Failure to open the jaw and mouth during phonation.

A faulty concept of what a truly open position feels like.

A faulty concept of resonance, which confuses what you hear inside your head with what you think others are hearing.

A subconscious attempt to save breath by not opening your mouth and throat—in effect "pinching the neck."

Side effects   Distorted, flattened vowels and unclear diction.

Piercing, shrill tone quality, particularly in loud dynamics.

Very limited resonance.

What to do

1. Review Lesson 11 thoroughly. Perform all the Class Activities again and drill the exercises.

2. While watching yourself in a mirror, sing the open vowels AH, AW, and OH. Do your habits make you start to close your jaw as soon as you start to sing? Try to prevent such closing, while maintaining full breath support and resonance.

3. In a familiar song, mark every AH and AW sound in red pencil. Then sing the song before your mirror, noting what you do at each of the marked sounds. If your jaw is in a closed position, sing the song several times more, consciously opening wide for each of those sounds. Notice the changes in tone quality that this produces.

CLASS ACTIVITIES

Using the exploratory exercises suggested above, survey all class members for evidences of the problems discussed. A useful outcome of this activity is to confirm for individuals that they do *not* have the particular problem being considered. This detailed examination will also help those whose singing displays any of the faults and will increase general sensitivity, by contrast, to the nature and sound of fault-free tone production.

Learning Musicianship

Singers sing *music*. To accomplish musical results with their voices they must be able to use musical materials accurately and skillfully, just as competent instrumentalists do.

Before a singer can perform in a truly meaningful, expressive way, the skills of musicianship must be mastered. While there is not adequate time in a voice class to give thorough training in these skills, you need to become aware of the techniques of musicianship that you will need in order to become an accomplished singer. Too often singers allow themselves to be lulled into thinking they can "get by" because they have a good ear for music and a quick ability to learn by imitation. With such talents, they feel, they do not need to go to the trouble of acquiring the somewhat technical skills of real musicianship. *Such a belief is a firm guarantee of limited success in any serious singing endeavor they may aspire to master.*

The purpose of Step 7 is to outline the most fundamental skills of musicianship that you will need as a singer, so that you may assess your present progress. In the long run these skills are as important as purely vocal accomplishments to your satisfaction and success in singing.

CONTENTS OF STEP 7

Lesson 26   **What Is Accuracy in Singing?**
Musicianship as the ability to use musical materials accurately; what accuracy in music is; in what ways it can be understood and evaluated; how the singer learns to master it.

Lesson 27   **Reading Notation: The Fundamental Musical Skill**
The singer's urgent need for music-reading ability; specific areas of skill that must be mastered.

LESSON 26

What Is Accuracy in Singing?

CONCEPTS

It may seem to you that in singing there are more ways to be wrong than to be right. As you struggle with persistent problems you may feel that about all you have learned is a long list of things that *won't* work. But what do *right* and *wrong* mean in singing? If they are taken to indicate something about how accurate you are, which is a common interpretation, then you need an understanding of what accuracy in singing involves. In the mathematician's tidy "2 + 2 = 4," any other answer is automatically inaccurate; by contrast, singing calls for several different, simultaneous answers or ways of being accurate.

You don't have to be told that sloppy singing is inaccurate, because its wrongness, or inaccuracy, is so obvious. You may even have heard reasonably effective singing that was marred by small inaccuracies, thus demonstrating clearly that many things must be correct at the same time if singing is to be heard as completely accurate in the broadest sense. Yet one of the most attractive qualities of fine singing is that it embodies just that sense of complete accuracy.

The dictionary defines *accurate* as "executed with care; exact, precise, or conforming to a standard." Notice that it says nothing about right or wrong. That is important if you've thought of such words as meaningful explanations of accuracy. The dictionary definition sheds a different light on what is expected of you when you try to produce an accurate singing performance. It expands the concept of accuracy to include the many, varied components of singing that must be produced with precision, careful execution, and attention to established standards.

Here is a list of components of a singing performance that can be evaluated in terms of an executed-with-care accuracy. Notice that such execution assumes that the care is exercised *every time;* nothing is fixed, final, or once-and-for-all accurate. Each time you sing you must re-create the accuracy for that performance. It would be impossible to evaluate the degree of accuracy of these components on any sort of mathematical scale, but fine singing will always show recognizable evidences of careful execution in these areas.

Singing Components that Can Be Evaluated for Accuracy

Conceptual Components   Strength of motivation: Does your singing show desire and enthusiastic personal involvement, or is it mechanical and lifeless?

	Clarity of concepts: Does your singing convey the impression that you have distinct ideas about what you want the audience to understand?
Vocal Components	Breath control: Does it give coordinated support to tone production or weaken it?
	Tone quality: Is it natural, well placed, clear, easy, and attractive?
	Resonance and projection: Are they consistent, natural, and easy?
	Legato technique: Do you sing a smooth, flowing line or not?
Textual Components	Color and placement of vowels and diphthongs.
	Precision and articulation of consonants.
	Word accents, phrasing, and clarity of word meaning.
	Pronunciation and enunciation of the language being sung.
	Coordination of word and musical meanings.
Musical Components	Facility in the control of basic music elements: rhythm, meter, and tempo; pitch, intervals, and scale patterns; tonality, major–minor relationships, harmony generally; intonation.
	Communication of the meanings of the musical score: staff, clefs, key signatures, dynamic markings, rhythmic markings, accents, phrasing, expressive markings, repeats, and special markings.
Personal Components	Ability to project a feeling of poise and control.
	Personal appearance: posture, facial expressions, mannerisms, dress.
	Use of a personal, individual style; charisma.

While many of these components are drawn from lessons already studied, others point ahead into the realm of expressive singing. Taken together, they stress the theme of *musicianship*: that singing is a musical activity first, in which your technical knowledge and skill are devoted to producing a musical result. If it is allowed to become mere entertainment, flashy exhibition, or uncontrolled "interpretation," it will always fall short in the degree of satisfaction it can provide. In general, the more accurate a performance is in terms of the components listed above, the more "musicianly" it will be.

CLASS ACTIVITIES

1.   The class will simulate a vocal contest or judged recital; those not singing will act as a panel of judges evaluating each singer's performance. Concentrate on the components listed in this lesson and hold class critiques after each person sings. Call attention to components that seem to be executed with care and that seem to be ignored or performed poorly. Every class member should contribute to the evaluation.

2.   Class members will record songs they have prepared for testing or recital, singing for the class as their performance is taped. When the tape is played back, hold personal and class evaluations similar to those in Activity 1. Be as objective and specific as possible, noting which components worked well as well as which ones were faulty. Try to discover causes for the faults in your own performance.

ON YOUR OWN

1.   Choose a song from this book or from elsewhere that you do not know at all. Study the score carefully, making a detailed list of every symbol or marking you do not understand. Assume the song was assigned to you to learn for class performance, so that you will have to demonstrate you

know what those markings mean. How does this affect your understanding of what learning the song would force you to do?

2.   Study a performance by a great singer on recordings or television, with the music score in front of you. Evaluate the performance in the way outlined in Class Activity 1. Note strengths or weaknesses in what the artist does; note whether or not he or she is executing with care. Do television performers use visual gimmickry to gloss over performance components that are *not* executed with care?

LESSON 27

Reading Notation: The Fundamental Musical Skill

CONCEPTS

If you couldn't read, you'd have trouble getting along in this complex world. Even though you might get a lot of information from radio and television, someone else would have to read you such things as road signs, menus, your paycheck, prices in stores, and a lot of things you now take for granted.

The singer who can't read music is in a similar position musically. True, a lot of musical information can be obtained by ear, but it is always limited to what other people "tell" you by making musical sounds for you to imitate. When your learning is restricted to such imitation, you sing *their* melodies, *their* rhythms, *their* phrasing, and *their* meanings. And what if they are wrong?

Learning to read music notation is the first step toward *musicianship,* which is *the ability to use musical materials accurately.* Singers who desire real satisfaction from their singing soon learn the value of looking at the notes. Like those learning to play instruments, vocalists discover that the most efficient way to use their own instrument—the voice—is to make their music by following the directions that notation gives them. In contrast to those who must still imitate others, they are freed to do it for themselves.

It cannot be denied that skilled music reading is a complex process, but so is reading the newspaper. Any reading ability is better than none, and it is far more productive to be able to read *some* music than to be complacently willing just to "get it by ear." In addition, you will soon find that each notational skill you master helps you use your vocal skills with more certainty and expressive control, just because you are more aware of what the notation says you should do.

Here is a list of five skill areas in reading notation, in the approximate order of their importance to the singer. Each of these details specific things you learn by *doing, paying attention, and practicing regularly.* They are not at all mysterious, and while they involve technical material they are clearly understandable. In every case the skill involves knowing what the symbols are, and then knowing what to do to convert the symbols into musical sounds. Think about it. That is exactly what you do when you read a line of words out loud. You recognize symbols—the words—and as a result you produce specific, controlled sequences of sound that represent the words. Music reading simply adds controlled pitch, tone quality, and rhythm to the sounds you already make.

Five Skill Areas in Notation Reading

1. *Use of rhythmic notation*—(learn to count!)
   Rhythmic note values
   Rests
   Measures (bars)
   Meter signatures
   Tempo markings
   Tempo changes
   Relationships among meter, rhythm, and tempo

2. *Use of pitch notation.*
   Letter names for notes
   Intervals: recognition of all intervals, read either up or down, by both appearance and sound
   Functions of sharps, flats, and naturals

3. *Use of harmonic patterns.*
   Keys and key signatures
   Concept of tonality
   Major–minor relationships
   Triads and other chords
   Cadences and their relation to melodic patterns

4. *Use of staff symbols.*
   Names of lines and spaces
   Clefs; specific notation for each
   Ledger lines
   Bar lines

5. *Use of expressive and interpretive notation.*
   Dynamics
   Phrasing
   Symbols for mood, emotional coloration
   Breathing marks

Appendix 3 (pp. 149–64) examines each of these skill areas in greater detail, supplying essential information and practical ways to learn the skills. Your instructor will determine how this material will be used in this class. Since time is limited, a voice class cannot be expected to teach real proficiency in music reading; the emphasis here must be on vocal skills. Music reading is a separate skill of considerable complexity, and specific training in it is strongly advised, in either another class or private coaching. Many useful habits leading to fluent music reading can be strengthened, however, in this class by careful study of the examples and exercises given and by using what you learn about music reading every time you sing a piece of music. When you study a new song, be sure you understand what every mark relating to the singer's line actually means that you should *do*. While it is valuable to be able to read the piano lines also, it is simply inexcusable not to understand what has been put there specifically for the singer.

When you don't understand a symbol, ask questions. Look it up. Write down the meaning you find. Then *use* it in singing the music the way it directs. This is exactly the way you learned to read language. While you were taught by parents and teachers, you also did a lot of trial-and-error experimentation with words as a child, until you were able to make the meaning clear to yourself and use the words on your own. One reason some people have trouble in reading music notation is that they don't take the time to do this kind of personal experimentation and learning on their own.

CLASS ACTIVITIES

1. The class will sing a familiar (or memorized) song together. Follow the music closely, as though you were seeing it for the first time. Check yourself to see if you are observing *every* printed marking—notes, words, dynamics, tempo, accents, fermatas, phrasings, breathing marks, expressive directions, and so on—put there to guide the singer. If you aren't, why not? Is it because you *chose* to do something different or simply because you overlooked that particular instruction? What difference would it make in your performance if you used it? Sing the song enough times to incorporate instructions you may not have been using.

2. As exercises, the class will use some of the drills and examples given in Appendix 3 for reading rhythms and intervals (pp. 151–57). When the technique of a particular example works well for the group, the class will transfer it to trying to read the melody of an unfamiliar song in the Song Collection. Refer to Seven Steps to Learning a New Song, Appendix 1, p. 145, for further suggestions.

3. The instructor will choose songs at random in a community songbook, and the class will "read" the melodies all together, without accompaniment. If you already know the tune, use your knowledge of it to guide your eye to see *all* the symbols given; that is, pay close attention to the notation itself, as though you were reading an unfamiliar melody. If the tune is unfamiliar, try to use everything you know about music reading—no matter how much or how little that is—in attempting to sing the melody *simply as a result of looking at the notation.* You may get help and encouragement from other class members who are better readers than you, and thus lead as the group sings together, but consciously try to make *your* reading be the result of what you see. A useful suggestion: Start by tapping the meter of the song with your foot while you clap the rhythm of the melody; then try to sing the pitches of the melody while you tap and clap.

ON YOUR OWN

Examine as many musical scores as you can find: popular sheet music, folksong books, symphony scores, choir music, hymn books, art songs—anything you can lay your hands on. Imagine that you have been assigned to perform that music in the immediate future. Sort out in your mind which parts of it make some sense to you and which parts are complete "Greek." Notice that the score's value to *you* is limited by the number of its components that you understand.

Making Singing Meaningful

The ultimate aim of voice training is expressive singing—interpreting music so that it is meaningful to those listening. This expands the concept of singing well beyond the mechanics and technical preliminaries about how the voice works that we have been dealing with and moves it into areas that depend on the personal involvement and unique individuality of the singer. The farther you go in this direction, the greater your need for personal instruction from a private voice teacher or coach. As we have pointed out, it is your voice, and it must be trained individually. Step 8 outlines the essentials of expressive, interpretive singing, to call attention in this class setting to the directions your voice training must take, but you must take increasing responsibility for finding the personalized instruction you need to enable your voice to sing in the way you want to be heard.

CONTENTS OF STEP 8

LESSON 28

What Is Interpretation?

CONCEPTS

If professional singers came to this class to sing one of the songs you have been working on, how would their interpretations differ from yours?

The question may not be as silly as it first seems. What do *you* understand as the meaning of *interpretation*? Is it a term you use to describe something you are really somewhat vague about? Could you clearly explain your understanding of it to someone not particularly interested in singing?

Fundamentally, of course, performance *is* interpretation. The dictionary defines *interpretation* as "rendering a musical composition according to one's own idea of the author's intention." By that definition, you interpret every time you sing.

This class has dealt primarily with specific techniques of the physical act of singing, and we have stressed that performance is a process of putting many of those techniques together in the same instant. The next step is to add to the physical techniques the emotional–intellectual elements of interpretation and expression.

Such elements are personal. In *your* singing they must be uniquely yours. To the mechanical-physical operations of the phonation machine that we have been studying you must begin to add your emotional reactions and intellectual understandings of what the music means. Your interpretation, in the broadest sense, will then represent exclusively you.

Some singers are badly misled at this point. They confuse a personal, charismatic "style" with interpretation. They have heard outstanding singers in the popular and concert fields who have developed such styles, and they mistakenly feel that the most direct route to their own interpretation is merely to imitate some successful singer. However, when they try to make such a style the substance of their own interpretation, they find the result quite unsatisfactory. The reason is simple: They are trying to "borrow" their interpretation from outside themselves, forgetting that true interpretation must come from within—"according to one's own idea," as the dictionary put it.

Interpretation starts with the musical score and its meanings. The printed music specifies what you must understand, react to, and be able to convert into musical sound. It represents the composer's intentions in a variety of ways, including notes, rhythms, words, dynamics, phrasing, expressive nuances, and special effects. Your interpretation of these elements begins with your ability to understand and translate the printed symbols into vocal sounds. The following checklist outlines areas in which that ability must be used competently.

Checklist of Knowledge and Skills Needed for Interpretive Singing

1. *Knowledge about the music.*

   a. What is the musical style?

   b. Is there a tradition about how it should be sung? How will this affect your performance?

   c. Who was the composer? What styles of music is he known for?

   d. Can you find out what the composer had in mind when writing this piece?

   e. What do the words mean? Can you make that meaning clear to the audience?

   f. If the piece is in another language, do you know the literal translation of the words in English?

   g. Is there a predominant mood in the music? In the words? Do they agree?

   h. Is this piece taken from a larger work, such as an opera, musical comedy, or oratorio? Does this affect how you will sing it?

   i. Have you heard others perform the piece, so that you have a perspective on what it actually sounds like?

   j. Have you studied and listened to the accompaniment as well as your voice part? How does it affect what you will do?

2. *Skills of musicianship.*

   a. Do you know in what key you are singing?

   b. What are the highest and lowest tones you must sing?

   c. Is the tessitura high, medium, or low?

   d. What meter and tempo are specified? Do they change?

   e. Are there rhythmically difficult passages in the melody? Do rhythmic differences between voice and accompaniment present problems for the singer?

   f. Are there phrasing problems in the words? In the music? In combining the two?

   g. Are there problems of diction built into the text? What solutions have you worked out?

   h. Will intonation be a problem at any point in the melody?

   i. Are there problems of harmony or scale patterns that make the melody line more difficult to sing accurately?

   j. What dynamics does the score ask the singer to produce?

   k. Do you know the meaning of every expressive marking and direction printed for the singer?

   l. Have you noted the location of every fermata, breathing mark, accent, ritard, accelerando, and other such marking?

3. *Vocal control.*

   a. Is your breath control secure enough to give dependable support to tone production and phrasing?

   b. Is your legato technique secure enough to permit flexible phrasing?

   c. Is your control of tone quality certain enough to allow you to manage changes of mood, dynamic shifts, and alterations of tempo?

   d. Are your vowels and consonants accurate enough to be understood in the way you are trying to project them?

   e. Is your tone control consistent enough to permit you to convey your concepts of what the music means?

Each of these questions probes an area of singing about which you can start doing something immediately. At the outset your interpretation should be confined to the accurate accomplishment of the techniques the questions explore. On the basis of that accomplishment, you will later develop more subtle skills of taste, discrimination, and emotional refinement.

CLASS ACTIVITIES

Each person will learn Exercises 28.1 and 28.2 thoroughly, memorizing them if possible. *Poor Wayfarin' Stranger* (p. 282) or another song chosen by the instructor may also be used if time permits. Each person will then perform for the class as an exercise in interpreting. Each performance will be followed by a class critique based on the checklist given in this lesson, pointing out in detail what succeeded and what didn't. This activity is most valuable if everyone knows the same music, because everyone will have worked on the same challenges. In preparing for this performance the following steps are helpful:

1. Study the music carefully—its melody, mood, words, dynamics, phrasing, tempo, and special effects. Choose the tone quality you think will best convey to your audience the meanings you find in the music and words.

2. Practice singing the piece with the tone quality you chose. Then, for contrast, sing with different quality. Compare the two for effectiveness.

3. Learn the music accurately and thoroughly. Make sure you are observing every note, word sound, rhythm, dynamic, tempo, phrasing, and special effect just as it is marked. Are you actually doing what it says, or do you just *think* you are?

4. If you feel the piece has a particular mood, think carefully about how you will control your voice to project that mood to your audience. Projecting a mood is quite different from simply feeling it yourself.

5. When you perform for the class, concentrate on projecting the tones and mood you have practiced. In the critique, will your audience tell you they understood the meanings you intended to communicate—or something else?

Exercise 28.1. Make every marking affect the way you sing.

Exercise 28.2.

G. F. Handel

ON YOUR OWN

Watch singers on television or in live performances, and try to define exactly what they are doing to interpret their songs. If you feel the interpretation is effective and communicative, what did you hear and see that gave you that reaction? If they appeared dull, why? Pinpoint specific components of their performances that produced the results you observed—elements of musicianship, vocal control, ways of communicating mood, and so on.

LESSON 29

What Is Meaning in Singing?

CONCEPTS

When you hear someone sing well, you may feel that he or she has given an expressive, meaningful performance. Their singing communicated something that you could understand and enjoy—a mood, a story, humor, a sense of beauty, great vocal skill—in short, some *meaning*.

Your own singing may so far have shown you how difficult it can be to convey specific meanings in the way that seems so easy for the singers you see on television or in concert. Perhaps you have found that, in spite of your best efforts, what your audience understands when you sing is not quite what you set out to communicate.

The whole concept of meaning in singing is a delicate and elusive one. Like a unique flavor in fine food, it is a quality that is impossible to define precisely; but, if it is not present, the food—or the singing—will not have the desired effect. You must make constant efforts to control the physical act of singing so that it will deliver a specific concept of meaning and avoid communicating unwanted meanings springing from mistakes.

While we cannot supply a simple, tidy definition of meaning, the following principles may help you to construct your personal understanding of what is involved:

1. *What gets across to the audience is the meaning of a given performance*. This says that meaning is whatever is conveyed to those listening. Putting it that way may open up a perspective you hadn't thought about, for that "whatever" can include things you don't want to convey, such as dullness, boredom, inaccuracy, nervousness, the wrong mood, or lack of clarity. Naturally you hope that the listeners will understand just the desirable meanings you are trying to convey, but the other possibility is always present.

2. *The meaning of singing exists in time*. It happens in the instant of singing itself. It is a fleeting, complex pattern of concepts and actions that emerges from what the singer does and projects in that instant. What a piece meant the last time you sang it may or may not be the meaning it will have this time. An old maxim says: "You never step in the same river twice"—meaning that before you can put your foot down the second time the river has moved on and has a different shape. Trying to sing meaning is like that; what you mean this time changes what you will mean next time, just because you have already experienced it once. Each performance is new and has a slightly different mix of the various meanings it is possible to put into singing.

Here are several kinds of meaning that can be examined and controlled separately; for each, you can make specific preparations to project exactly the shades of meaning you want to sing.

Three Kinds of Meaning Used in Singing

1. *The meanings of the music.*

    a. Structure. How is the music put together? How does it use musical form, tonality, rhythm, melody, tempo, meter, consonance and dissonance, repetition and contrast, dynamics, and special effects?

    b. Performance requirements. What does the music demand of the singer in the way of tone control, breathing, tessitura, phrasing, vocal control, flexibility, projection, and musicianly skills?

2. *The meanings of the words.*

    a. Structure. Are the lyrics poetry or prose? Are they narrative, abstract commentary, or fantasy? Formal or idiomatic? In English or another language? Is their content hard to understand? Do they have a predominant mood?

    b. Performance requirements. What are the specific demands of the words in terms of pronunciation and enunciation? Vowel colors and diphthongs? Consonants? Tongue-twisters? What phrasing difficulties, obscure words, awkward sentence structures, and stilted meanings do they contain?

3. *Personal meanings supplied by the singer.*

    a. Visual meanings. What do the singer's appearance, posture, mannerisms, attitude, facial expressions, gestures, dress, grooming, poise, vitality, and confidence contribute to the meaning of the performance?

    b. Empathetic meanings. What nonverbal meanings are conveyed? Ability to project and sustain a mood? Ability to portray feelings and emotional shadings vocally? Apparent sincerity and personal involvement? By contrast, does the singer convey the ability to control negative meanings—that is, *not* to do things that convey wrong meanings?

    Remember, in singing performance, what your audience *gets* is the meaning.

CLASS ACTIVITIES

Each person will be asked to prepare a different song, learning it thoroughly. Before performing your song for the class, tell the meaning of the text using only your own words. Do not use any of the phrases of the song, and avoid the key words of the text. Even if the meaning seems obvious or simple, try to restate it in different terms. If it will help, invent a situation in which the idea of the words might logically be used. For the song *Take My Heart* (p. 232), for example, the rewording might go:

The song *Take My Heart* is being sung by a soldier to his girl as he leaves for war. They have had an argument, but in the emotion of leaving he sings to her, "Hold everything you love about me fresh in your mind. Remember the times you have calmed me down and listened to me gripe about the army. Quickly now—take me in your arms for one last kiss! Oh, yes, I know, we've argued, and I said some pretty nasty things about you, but you know I usually say only nice things, don't you? So, hold everything. . . ."

After each person has sung, the class will discuss whether the meaning of the words sung in the performance was made clearer by having heard the translation beforehand. If the song is sung in a language other than English, try to make the translation-explanation so specific that the audience can follow the meaning as it is sung in the original language.

ON YOUR OWN

1. Sing the song you know best before your mirror. Convey the meaning of the words and music to the best of your ability, as though there were an audience in front of you. Watch particularly for personal meanings you may be injecting without knowing it—bad posture, facial expressions, motions of the head, a constant frown, and so on. Can you see actual evidence that you are conveying the right mood and word meaning?

2. Prepare your own account of the words for a song that another class member will sing; compare your version with the one the other student reads to the class. Are there differences? How important are they? Discuss them with the other person.

LESSON 30

What Is Expression in Singing?

CONCEPTS

Singers are often heard to say that they want to "sing with expression," or "sing expressively." Such singing is seen as the goal of all their vocal training; it is what they want their voices to be able to do. We have assumed from the beginning that this is one of your vocal goals, too—but how clear is your understanding of what those phrases mean?

A workable definition might be: Singing expressively is the singer's act of conveying emotion, mood, and other nonverbal meanings through tone. The concept is often attached to the individuality of the singer—you express your*self*—which suggests that what is really being conveyed is the singer's personal concept of the emotion, mood, and meaning of the song.

This is particularly important when singing narrative or dramatic words, where your singing must convey specific word meanings related directly to the context. When a word has several possible meanings or emotional connotations, such as the word "love," your expressiveness in performance is essential. If you sing "I love you," then the meaning the audience receives depends on which of the various meanings of "love" you convey to them in the way you sing. If this expressive choice is not made and clearly understood, then what you sing will probably be heard as vague or meaningless.

Here are some suggestions about concepts, skills, and personal qualities that make expressive singing possible. At first these may seem too broad and vague to help you solve specific problems. If this is your reaction, it springs from the most basic problem about expression, which is that *the most important things music expresses cannot be explained in words.* Preparing yourself to sing expressively involves adding to the technical components of singing many vital ingredients that are purely emotional and nonverbal. The most expressive, emotional singing you will ever hear will evade your best efforts to describe it accurately with words, but you are certainly aware of its expressive content when you hear it sung by a skilled performer.

Some Sources of Expressive Singing

1. *Something to express.*

    a. You must understand the meanings of the song: music, words, style, tradition, mood, phrasing.

b. You must have developed insight into what can be expressed in singing and what cannot.

c. You need experience with emotional values and control. Do you have a mature perspective that allows you to know one emotion from another? What qualities of tone do you associate with various emotions and moods? Can you reproduce them by conscious choice?

2. *Dependable vocal control.*

a. You must have firmly established habits of correct tone production: posture, breathing, open phonation, adequate resonance and projection, correct vowel and consonant production, and legato technique.

b. You must sing with competent musicianship, using materials accurately and flexibly.

3. *Vitality and continual growth.*

a. You need to reevaluate your singing sounds constantly. Can you improve or modify them? What must you do to make changes? What do you learn from your mistakes?

b. You must let the music "age" in you. Good wine needs time to mature in oak barrels; similarly, what you sing should be given time to grow more meaningful in the solid timber of your experience. Constantly restudy the music you sing. Reexamine its structure, mood, and meanings for you. Assume that you will never reach the state of having completely learned the song; there is always something more to be done with it. Come back time and again to specific tones, phrases, words, and melodies that seem unsatisfactory to you. You never outgrow the need to refine and strengthen your fundamental vocal skills, because you are constantly growing as a person and a singer.

CLASS ACTIVITIES

Each person will prepare a new song for class performance, learning it thoroughly but not memorizing it. Use your song in the following ways with the rest of the class as an audience. If there is time to record and hold class critiques for each performance the activity will increase in value.

1. Read the words aloud, as though to an audience of hundreds. Be an actor. Convey meaning and expressive values in the way you read. What do the words say? It may help to build narrative situations around the words, as you did for *Take My Heart* in Lesson 29. Attach emotional shadings to the words if possible; for example, read them as though they made you sad, angry, happy, and so on. If the words are poetry, don't get trapped by the rhyme patterns into reading in a singsong manner.

2. Ask your audience to give back to you the principal meanings and expressive values they understood from what you did. Are they the ones you intended? If not, can you discover what made the difference?

3. Try reading the words aloud with a contrasting mood or emotional tone. Can you maintain one level of expression throughout?

4. Sing the song, doing your best to convey the same meanings and expressive qualities you read aloud in either 1 or 3 above. As much as you can, make your singing say the meanings in the way the words alone did. Observe specific difficulties you encounter in trying to do this.

ON YOUR OWN

1. In preparation for the Class Activities of this lesson, perform all of the activities before your mirror. Watch your singing activity closely. Does your reflection in the mirror actually communicate the meanings and expressive qualities you feel the song calls for? Can you make the communication work a little better when you are only reading the words aloud? Don't be afraid to

ham it up a little, but watch carefully what happens to your appearance and the sound of your voice when you do.

2.   As a parallel activity, read a newspaper story before your mirror, pretending that you are a famous television newscaster. Make it dramatic and intense. Remember, *understanding* the meaning of what you read is quite different from being able to *communicate* that meaning to others. Can you make the latter happen very clearly in reading to your mirror image?

LESSON 31

Mood as an Expressive Tool

CONCEPTS

If we say "Sing your song expressively!" you may respond by trying to project a mood that seems to you to fit the meaning of the words and music. *Mood* is defined as "a state of mind in which an emotion or set of emotions gains ascendancy." Since expression is usually associated with emotion, the idea of mood provides a handy device with which to organize related emotions around a central theme that you want your singing to convey.

The problem is, of course, that it is not always possible to make singing convey a *specific* mood to someone else. There are too many subtle shadings of mood available, and your voice can produce an amazing number of tonal colors. Finding the exact combination of moods and tones that will transfer what you are experiencing into someone else's consciousness is a rare achievement. Nevertheless, if your singing is to be meaningfully expressive, you must at least suggest distinct areas of mood-emotion that your listeners can recognize and relate to the music they hear you singing.

You use such areas naturally when you speak. Your voice responds to the dominant emotions of a mood by using tone qualities and dynamics that are generally associated with those emotional shadings. For example, when you are happy or excited your tone is usually bright and loud; sadness or solemnity usually evokes quieter, darker tones. The number and variety of shadings that you use without conscious thought are very great indeed.

Table 31.1 lists some of the more obvious mood-emotion areas. As you study them you will find that you already associate certain tone qualities with many of their dominant emotions. You should also notice that these emotions usually have varied meanings, particularly when you combine them in the mood with which they are associated. Emotions rarely occur singly; they overlap and mingle. As you explore this subject to enlarge and broaden your repertoire of mood-emotions, you need to discover consistent tone qualities that you associate with each emotion. This assumes, of course, that you understand what the emotion *is,* for until you do you have no way of responding to it tonally. It is precisely that understanding that you have to convey to others if your singing is to project recognizable moods expressively. Developing such a repertoire of mood-emotions is a vital part of the process of letting music "age" in you (which we discussed in Lesson 30). The truest understanding of an emotion comes from experiencing it. In addition, it will be useful to study both a dictionary and a thesaurus in your search for exact meanings and relationships.

There are many more. The more expressively you are able to sing, the longer your personal list will become. Both the words and the music of expressive songs draw on various of these emotional shadings. To sing such pieces successfully you must first discern which emotions are

Table 31.1. Some Representative Areas of Mood-Emotions

Mood Area	Typical Related Emotions
Happiness	Joy, delight, elation, gladness, cheerfulness, humor, laughter, enthusiasm, jubilation, animation
Sadness	Sorrow, grief, woe, anguish, despair, mourning, weeping, crying, gloom, dejection, despondency
Excitement	Exhilaration, effervescence, ebullience, thrills, fever pitch, turmoil, agitation
Courage	Bravery, strength, valor, nerve, boldness, inspiration, fortitude, heroism, daring
Anger	Fury, rage, wrath, temper, indignation, ire, revenge, bitterness, rancor
Fear	Panic, worry, dread, terror, horror, alarm, fright, doom, trembling
Love	Affection, tenderness, devotion, yearning, delicacy, gentleness, sentimentality
Hatred	Hostility, detestation, animosity, scorn, loathing, malice, contempt
Reverence	Awe, wonder, veneration, religious zeal, humility, deference, respect, solemnity

present or implied and then produce the tones and other performance techniques that will communicate them. Here are some useful first steps toward that goal:

1. *Examine what your speaking voice does to project emotions.* When you have a clear concept of what a particular emotion is, what kind of tone do you use in speaking about it? You will probably find it more natural to talk about an emotion than to sing about it, at least in the beginning. When you do speak about it, listen closely to the tone itself, and try to define (and then, of course, remember) its unique qualities of color, dynamics, and inflection. When you have assigned a particular emotion to the song you are going to sing, read the words aloud with a tone that you feel matches the emotion. Then sing the song, trying to give the singing tone the same emotional quality. Such comparisons will help you to build a usable vocabulary of mood-emotion tones.

2. *Study other performance components you use to project mood.* Among these will be *tempo* (faster for happy and excited moods; slower for sad, reverent, and fearful moods); *dynamics* (soft for sadness, love, and reverence; loud for happiness, anger, and excitement); *facial expressions* (you rarely sing "deadpan," if you are expressive); *gestures;* and *accents* of various sorts for emphasis. Becoming aware of what you do with such components will subconsciously help you choose and sing the most appropriate tone quality, because it helps you become more completely involved in projecting one specific mood. Your whole singing effort is directed toward that one objective.

3. *Remember that mood happens in time and must be continuous and sustained.* An old saying warns that "a fence is only as strong as its weakest post." The same idea can be applied to singing a mood convincingly. For your listeners to understand and appreciate the mood you are trying to sing, they must hear it all through the phrases and lines you sing. Your legato technique and habit of phrasing to make sense must be so secure that you will not let the mood break down or unthinkingly insert any tones that are out of the mood.

CLASS ACTIVITIES

Exercises 31.1 and 31.2 are contrasting musical settings of the couplet used in Lesson 22 to study phrasing (p. 91). In preparation for this activity, restudy that lesson, and note again how many varied meanings it was possible to read into the couplet simply by altering the phrasing. This activity builds on that variety by asking you to add further meanings implied by specific moods.

Learn the musical settings in the two exercises thoroughly, so that you can sing each one accurately and with confidence. Each person will then be asked to sing one or both of them for the class, trying to project a specific mood suggested by the instructor immediately before the singer begins. Moods that work well include sadness, extreme happiness, anger, dreaminess or romantic love, and the other representative moods in Table 31.1.

Exercise 31.1. You supply the tempo and dynamics.

Low key

Exercise 31.1.

High key, piano part

Exercise 31.2.   Slow and sustained.

I fear _____ my love _____ may

kiss and tell, _____ kiss and

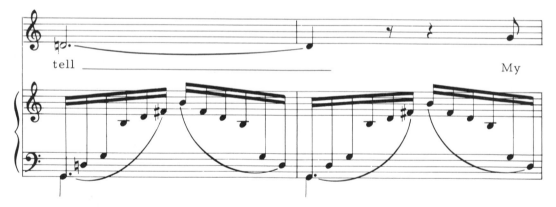

tell _____ My

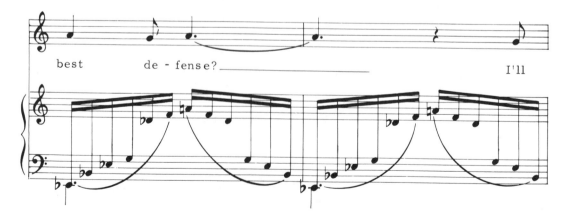

best de - fense? _____ I'll

           STEP 8 MAKING SINGING MEANINGFUL

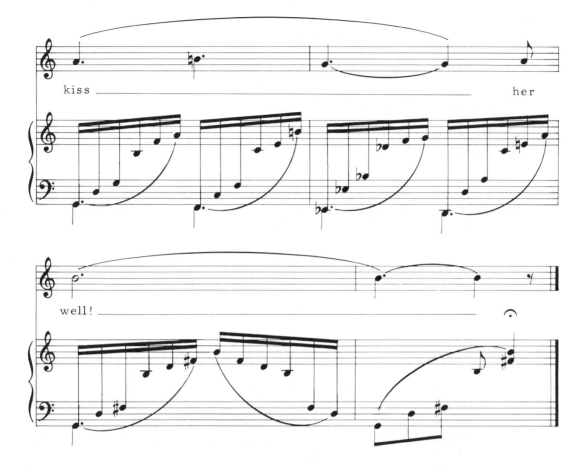

kiss _____ her

well! _____

After each person sings, the class will hold a discussion about the following questions, encouraging the expression of as many contrasting viewpoints as possible, since this underscores the wide variety of reactions a singer may expect from an audience.

1.   Did the singer succeed in conveying to you, the listener, the mood that was assigned? If not, why not?

2.   How did the mood or meaning of the music itself, as distinct from the words, relate to the assigned mood? Did it agree, conflict, or have no connection?

3.   How much of the singer's communication of mood depended on *visual* aspects of performance, such as gestures, facial expressions, or posture, and how much on *audible* aspects, such as tone quality, dynamics, diction, and inflection?

4.   Did the singer have to modify the music in any way to achieve the assigned mood? Was it necessary to change the specified tempo, dynamics, or phrasing?

5.   Can you pinpoint exactly how the singer managed to convey whatever mood you understood him or her to be singing?

LESSON 32

Dynamics as Expressive Tools

CONCEPTS

What determines how loudly you speak in normal conversation?

Such factors as whether you are speaking to one person or many and how far away they are obviously are important. In addition, what are talking about and the mood of the conversation have an influence. You speak softly for intense, intimate, or sad meanings and louder for joyous, excited, or angry feelings.

Singing uses similar controls. However, their use is complicated by the need to sing a continuous vocal line and the fact that the score often specifies exactly how loudly the music should be sung. Because you do have to sing a sustained tone, it may seem difficult to produce different dynamic levels. Also, problems in vocal technique, such as difficulty singing high tones softly or low tones loudly, may get in the way.

The composer specifies the dynamics he or she had in mind by using dynamic symbols, which are placed above the notes and words in the score. The most frequently used symbols are listed in Appendix 3, pp. 163–64. These symbols have been compared to road signs, which tell you how to travel along the main road of the music itself—the melody, rhythm, and words. If you habitually focus all your attention on the road, you may not even *see* the road signs, so your singing won't include many dynamic shadings.

In speaking, you use dynamic shadings to convey subtleties of meaning; you call them *inflections*. These come to you naturally, as part of the meaning you want to speak, so that you rarely speak in a monotone, all at the same level of loudness. The process of singing dynamics in music is based on transferring this habit into the production of singing tone. Here are some suggestions that may help you in making that transfer work. They restate and reassemble components of singing that we have already dealt with to some extent, but this time the focus is on ways of training you to control dynamic shadings in your singing.

1. *Discipline yourself to notice dynamic symbols*. This is where the process starts. When you look at music you probably now see the words and notes first. Do the dynamic markings catch your eye? They are just as much parts of the music you are to sing as the words and notes and should be seen at the same time. A good way to train yourself in this habit is to circle each dynamic marking in red in your score, so that your eye will pick it up the next time through. Too often, singers pay attention to dynamics only after someone points out to them that they have sung a piece too softly or too loudly according to what the music says.

2. *Know what the symbols mean and how you control your voice to perform them.* Study pp. 163–64 carefully, and look up every symbol you don't understand in the song you are working on. By using the exercises of this lesson, and some personal experimentation, find out how you sing the various dynamic levels and change from one to another. Unless the symbols can trigger a correct response in the way you sing, you will, in effect, "miss the road sign," and it will have been of no value to the way you perform the music. Usually this means that you simply won't produce the expressive effect the composer had in mind.

3. *Decide which dynamics best convey the meanings of the piece you are singing.* In addition to studying what the composer wrote down, think about the mood, phrasing, and other meanings of the words and melody, and make your own decision about the most appropriate dynamics to sing. Above all, don't ignore this area and try to sing the song without any attention to dynamic levels. This usually leads to singing everything too loudly, in a monotonous, unexpressive manner.

4. *Always sing your best tone—deeply supported, open, clear, and resonant.* Such tone production is the only kind in which dynamic shadings will consistently work. Lesson 1 noted that singing should feel good. The more completely this best tone becomes the only kind you produce, the truer that statement becomes. The good feeling you get about vital tone is an emotional-physical reaction that is closely allied to dynamic expressiveness. You can prove this to yourself by speaking or singing several lines in a monotone. The longer you do it, the less vital and resonant the tone becomes, simply because it sounds—and feels—dull, uninteresting, and lifeless. Then speak or sing the same passage with a dynamically flexible, resonant tone, and notice how much more vital it sounds and feels at once.

CLASS ACTIVITIES

1. The class will sing together each of the dynamic levels of the following chart on the tone G. Think of the top level, *ff,* as the loudest tone you can sing with complete vocal control and the bottom level, *pp,* as the softest. Try to develop a consistent feeling and sound for each level as you sing it. For variety, one person will point at different levels at random while the class tries to sing those levels immediately. Use a variety of vowels.

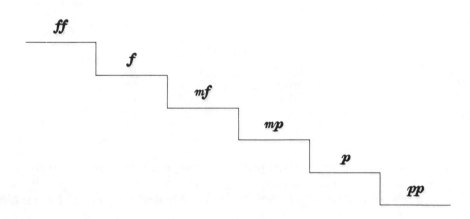

2. The class will sing Exercises 32.1–32.3 as a class, in smaller groups, and individually, using as many different dynamic levels and vowel colors as time permits. Use the following checklist to evaluate the effectiveness of your dynamic control:
    a. Does seeing the dynamic symbol cause an immediate response in your singing?
    b. Do you sing a consistent volume each time you see the symbol?
    c. Do you know the exact meaning of every symbol in the exercise?
    d. Do you sing your best tone at every dynamic level?

e. Are higher tones hard for you to sing softly? If so, why?

f. Are lower tones hard for you to sing loudly? If so, why?

g. Do you tend to strain, sing a breathy tone, or lose resonance while you sing changing dynamic levels (*crescendo* and *diminuendo*)?

Exercise 32.1.

(a) *Sing* **pp** ——————— *ff*
(b) *Sing* *ff* ——————— *pp*

Exercise 32.2.
Transpose up and down as desired. Be sure the top and bottom tones are the same loudness on (a) through (d).

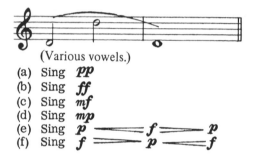

(Various vowels.)

(a) Sing **pp**
(b) Sing *ff*
(c) Sing *mf*
(d) Sing *mp*
(e) Sing *p* ——— *f* ——— *p*
(f) Sing *f* ——— *p* ——— *f*

Exercise 32.3.
Sing one consistent dynamic level for the entire line, even though you are changing vowels.

MAH_____   MOH_____   MAH_____
MEE_____   MAH_____   MOO_____
MEH_____   MIH_____   MEE_____

Sing the entire line (a) *f* (b) *p* (c) *ff* (d) *pp*

3. Sing a very familiar song for the class, preferably from memory. Have class members follow the score closely, noting what happens in your singing at each dynamic marking in the score. In the critique that follows your singing, be prepared to explain anything you did that was different from what the score said.

4. Change every dynamic symbol in a familiar song. Make these dynamic changes represent as different an idea of the song's meaning as possible. Remember the line you read in Lesson 31 as though you were angry, sad, and so on? Apply that method here. Sing the song using the new dynamics. What does this do to the total meaning? How does your audience react to the new interpretation? How did it change your tone?

ON YOUR OWN

Listen to several different singers on recordings, radio, or television. Include as many musical styles as possible. Observe the use each makes of dynamics. Do some tend to ignore dynamic shading altogether? Do some sing too loudly all the time or too softly? Is there any relation between the security of their tone and the way they use dynamics? Do the singers you feel to be most expressive in their performances make consistent use of dynamic shadings?

LESSON 33

Tempo as an Expressive Tool

CONCEPTS

How do you tell whether you are singing a song too quickly, too slowly, or about right?

If your music includes one of the tempo marks listed in Appendix 3 (p. 162), you should be able to answer that question. But exactly how fast do you go for each of those marks? How fast is *Presto? Andante? Largo?* If you sing too slowly, the music will sound lifeless and dull, but if you go too quickly it will sound rushed, nervous, and inaccurate. How do you find the right tempo?

There is probably no single, completely "right" tempo for any particular piece, since there are so many elements of tempo to be considered. Better terms would be *appropriate* or *suitable*— that is, appropriate and suitable for the particular performance *you* are doing. As the performer, you determine each time just how fast you will actually sing. The musical score gives suggestions and instructions in the tempo marks, but *you* are doing the singing, so those marks can be only as meaningful as your singing makes them.

In spite of this apparent uncertainty, there are certain guiding principles you can use to find the tempo best suited to your performance. Here are some of the most basic:

1. *Develop and refine your inner sense of rate of speed.* Music is measured by patterns of beats that move at specified rates of speed. Your inner sense of what fast, moderate, and slow rates actually *feel like* needs to be trained and refined through practice and continuous attention to musical performance. The use of metronome speeds (see 3 below) is a good way to begin, but the objective always is to develop a *sense* of how fast you are going—an "inner clock"—that gives you personal control of tempo without the need for external guidance.

2. *Know the meanings of the standard tempo marks.* Most tempo marks are in Italian or German, and many are used only occasionally for special expressive effects. To help your performance, you need to look up the meanings of the marks you don't know and write their meanings in English right in your music. Such tempo marks are another kind of "road sign" that gives directions about how you are to move along the main road of the music. The fact that they are not always in plain terms you already understand does not lessen their importance. If you drive a car in Europe you are expected to obey the road signs even though they are not in English.

3. *Use metronome markings if they are given.* The metronome was invented in the early nineteenth century as a mechanical means of measuring how many musical beats occur in one minute.

Indications of this measurement are now printed in many scores, often in connection with the tempo mark. Some examples are:

Adagio (♩ = 60) sixty quarter notes per minute, or one per second

Andante (♩ = 84) eighty-four half notes per minute

Vivace (♪ = 144) one hundred forty-four eighth notes per minute

Unless there is some instruction to the contrary, the note given in the metronome marking is the one that gets the beat. Since these metronome marks establish a precise, measurable rate of speed, they provide part of the answer to the question about the "right" tempo. If the composer actually designated them (rather than an editor or arranger), they are right in the sense that they are authoritative. But, since you won't have a metronome ticking beside you when you perform, you must develop your own rate-of-speed sense if you are to conform to the composer's intentions.

4. *Let the shortest notes set the tempo.* You won't be able to sing a piece any faster than the rate of speed at which you can sing the shortest notes clearly. For example, the figure ♪. ♪ (a dotted thirty-second note and a sixty-fourth note) in a tempo marked "*Presto* ♩ = 160" would be impossible to sing, for it would call for 2,560 sixty-fourth notes per minute, or roughly 43 per second, a speed far faster than anyone could sing them. If the same figure appeared in a tempo marked "*Largo* ♪ = 40," they could be sung easily, for there would be only about five sixty-fourth notes per second. As you study a new song to determine the best tempo for your performance, find the shortest notes and choose a tempo that lets you sing them clearly and easily.

5. *Examine the difficulty of the text.* If the words include tongue twisters—difficult combinations of consonants and vowels—your tempo must be slow enough to allow you to wrap your tongue around them. If your song contained, for example, the line, "The Lord's wrath blasts through the enemy's hosts with flames and frosts!" you would have real difficulty singing it rapidly. Try it. Sometimes lines of vowels with few consonants can be just as tricky. Try to say or sing, "How are our errors?" several times rapidly.

6. *Examine the mood and meaning of the words and music.* The most appropriate tempo is often quite clearly suggested by the mood of a piece. Sadness, solemnity, and dignity seem to call for broader, slower tempos, while happiness and excitement demand faster paces. If the tempo you choose will not let the meaning of the words come through to your audience, because it is either too fast or too slow, it should clearly be changed. In this expressive realm, you are called on to develop and use your best judgment.

CLASS ACTIVITIES

1. On a signal from the instructor, close your eyes and count silently at the rate of one count per second; make no sound of any sort. At count 30, clap once. The instructor will watch a clock and indicate exactly when 30 seconds have elapsed. How close did you get? Can you adjust your mental rate and get closer on the second and third tries?

2. Use the same technique for other metronome markings indicated by your instructor. Start with divisions or multiples of the one-per-second rate, such as ♩ = 120 or ♩ = 180; as soon as possible try unrelated tempos such as ♩ = 72, ♩ = 100, and ♩ = 48. If possible, have a metronome available for finding out how accurate you were—*after* you have tried the rate by yourself.

ON YOUR OWN

1. Make a game of setting tempos in your mind. Come back to it often, for short periods of time. Begin with tempos you can check, such as multiples of the one-per-second rate, which you can compare with the second hand of your watch. Other tempos are usually associated with specific activities. For instance, normal marching tempo is ♩ = 120. A moderate walking speed is between ♩ = 72 and ♩ = 80. This is often call *andante,* which is derived from the Italian verb *andare,* to walk. See how much you can improve your sensitivity to rates of speed.

2. Read through unfamiliar songs that have metronome markings. Try to establish the rate yourself, and then check it with the metronome. When you read the song, do your best to keep going at the rate you have set, even though you may miss many notes.

3. Read other unfamiliar songs that have no metronome marks. Use the principles given in this lesson to establish the tempo.

Moving toward Artistry

Artistic performance is the ultimate goal of voice training. The term *artistic* cannot be exactly defined, but the quality of performance it describes is immediately recognizable as superior to any other kind. Step 9 examines some of the aspects of artistry that you need to understand and work toward. These aspects stress characteristics of an artistic performance that can be observed and studied separately. They demonstrate that performing artistically is the summation of all the technical and expressive vocal techniques this book has explored.

CONTENTS OF STEP 9

LESSON 34

What Is Artistic Singing?

CONCEPTS

If someone asked you to explain *artistic singing,* what would you tell them? What is the "art" of singing?

The dictionary defines *art* as "skill in performance, acquired by experience, study, or observation," and adds that it involves "the conscious use of skill, taste, and creative imagination in the production of aesthetic objects." This book has been concerned with helping you acquire skills of performance through study and experience. The final step, that of developing taste and creative imagination, is one that each individual must finally take for herself or himself; there are few how-to rules that can be written out or that apply generally.

If you like coffee, the smell of it being freshly brewed is one of life's better experiences. But could you define that smell with words? You are quite aware of it when it is present, and you probably understand a variety of meanings when you smell it, but you couldn't adequately tell anyone else—with words alone—what those meanings are.

It is no accident that the appreciation of aesthetic values is often called *taste,* for it is an experience similar to tasting fine food or smelling fresh coffee. It is something you do without defining, and it is based squarely on your sensitivity to nonverbal values and ideas. Such values are delicate and fragile, yet they are clear and unmistakable to the receptive mind. That receptivity is the key; if your mental ear hears only precise, explicit word ideas, you may simply be unaware of subtle aesthetic values, somewhat as a person with a bad head cold is unable to smell coffee.

We cannot list Six Easy Steps to Artistry any more readily than you could explain the coffee smell. But we can point out that the coffee smell is the result of long preparation, including the activities of planting the tree, picking and drying the beans, blending, roasting, and grinding them, and storing them, all in a manner that will bring that smell to your coffee pot. In one way or another all those preparations stand behind the finished product whose scent gives you such pleasure.

Similarly, the way your singing artistry will flower depends on the care with which you have tended the plant of your musical-vocal preparation. Realizing this gives added purpose and importance to your technical training, because it lays a firm foundation for the expressive control that will lead you to artistic performance.

At the beginning we said that only you could supply the motivation needed for your singing. We have come full circle and can now point out that the impulse of that motivation must lead you to develop your taste and creative imagination as the final component needed to make your singing artistic. This class may have shown you how to prepare the soil and nurture your vocal plant well, as steps to bringing the buds of taste and imagination to flower. That is about all that teaching and lessons can do. The scent and color of that flowering must grow out of the unique person you are.

While it is impossible to tell you exactly how to produce artistry, we can enumerate several characteristics of an artistic performance that you can observe and use as guidelines in your own study of artistry.

Recognizable Characteristics of an Artistic Performance

1. *In artistic performance, technical accuracy is an independent, nonverbal value.* The various forms of accuracy discussed in Lesson 26 reach such a stage of perfection that they are heard clearly as separate communicative values in their own right. Listeners find real satisfaction in the fact that tone, diction, rhythm, pitch, dynamics, and other technical aspects of the music are exactly right. This accuracy is a powerful nonverbal product of artistic performance that is based squarely on adequate preparation.

2. *The artistic performance communicates.* You don't need to tell the coffee-lover that you've put the pot on, and you don't need to tell the sensitive listener, "This performance is artistic!" In both cases, the flavor comes through. The audience *hears* the artistry just as quickly as the coffee-lover smells the fragrance from the steaming pot. This instant communication is the end product of the performance concepts explored in Step 6.

3. *Artistry makes singing appear easy and natural.* A high-rise building towers above surrounding structures with graceful ease and beauty. It is obvious that it could not go so high without its rigid, angular steel frame, but the framework is not what impresses you about the building's appearance. Similarly, the artistry of fine singing cloaks the framework of technical skills needed to produce it. The surest evidence of great technique is that the result usually appears to be so simple—that is, untechnical—that "anyone can do it!" The more complete your own control of technique becomes, the more fully you will understand not only why just anyone can *not* do it but also why it must appear that anyone can.

4. *The impact of artistic singing is chiefly emotional.* What terms describe an artistic performance? Such words as beautiful, moving, wonderful, pure, delicate, expressive, and colorful are often used, revealing a primarily emotional response to what was heard. From the beginning we have said that emotion is a vital component of singing, from that first "want to" all the way to the finished performance. It is logical that a performance will present emotional values in their most refined forms.

5. *Artistic singing always sounds new, fresh, and vital.* What is the difference between the smell of the coffee while it is being brewed and its fragrance two hours later? When it is being reheated, it is still coffee—same liquid, same color—but its most pleasing aspect has flown away. Similarly, the artistic performance never sounds "warmed over." The artistry consists in making the music sound "freshly brewed," as though the performer were creating it right on the spot for the first and only time. This lends it excitement, vitality, and a fleeting quality of newness that, like the smell of coffee, is unique.

CLASS ACTIVITIES

1. As the final project for Step 9 and for this class, each student will plan and prepare a complete recital for a general audience. Sing from memory at least two contrasting numbers chosen to make a program that is balanced, pleasing, and, to the extent possible, artistic. Think about, discuss, and practice giving performances that demonstrate some of the characteristics listed in this lesson. Also study Lesson 35 carefully, and try to incorporate some of its suggestions in your performance. Choose music you think you can sing well and successfully.

Plan the recital thoroughly. Make it an "occasion" by inviting friends, parents, and the general public. Print programs. Serve refreshments. Present awards. In every way possible make it a special event.

2.   Attend live performances by singers. Begin with familiar styles, but include others also. Evaluate the singing in terms of this lesson. To what extent was it artistic? Where did it fail? Why? Can you pinpoint exactly what was missing? Does your attempt to make these judgments tell you anything about your own understanding of the concept of artistic performance?

ON YOUR OWN

Ask some friends who you feel have little appreciation of singing to let you explain to them your concept of artistic singing. Ask for their reactions about the following:

1.   Did your explanation make sense to them?

2.   Did the explanation tell them something about singing that they could understand even though they are not particularly musical?

3.   Did your explanation sound at all phony, artificial, or affected?

After you have their reactions, reexamine your ideas about artistic singing. Do you still think of it in vague terms, or have you been forced to clarify and organize your concepts?

LESSON 35

Stage Presence: Self-Consciousness Mastered

CONCEPTS

What has happened to your self-consciousness?

Lesson 2 began with the assumption that normally you feel self-conscious when you sing for others, and we suggested ways of learning to control that feeling. If these have been effective, you should now at least be aware of the other side of the coin of self-consciousness, which is *stage presence*.

When you were troubled by all those eyes watching you, you were self-conscious in the sense of being afraid of what *might* happen. Stage presence, by contrast, gives you self-conscious command of a performance situation, which grows out of your confidence in what you can do. The fact that people are watching you becomes a welcome opportunity to communicate with them. This transforms your awareness of yourself from fear of failure to confidence of success. You know you can control what *will* happen.

Like the development of artistry, stage presence results from growth and maturity. The skills you have acquired give you confidence. Greater comprehension of what singing involves provides you with more meanings to convey. Your broadening knowledge of yourself has revealed that many of the things you feared might happen really won't, because they are products of your imagination. You have experienced the exhilarating sensation of dominating a human situation for a brief time as the Performer. Most basically, of course, you have confirmed the fact that *you really like to sing for others*.

This doesn't mean that you are never nervous or that you will always feel complete assurance about performing. The resilient tensions of performance will probably continue to raise your pulse rate a little. However, the benefits of stage presence will give increasing support to what you are trying to do and thus improve your success rate. Here are some characteristics of a performance dominated by stage presence:

1. *You sing to your audience, not at them.* This is one of the ultimate skills of performance. It transforms singing into real person-to-person communication. What is your reaction when someone talks to you without ever looking at you? You may feel that he or she is avoiding you, is nervous or uncertain, or perhaps even wishes you would go away. Audiences react in similar ways when singers look at the floor or ceiling, stare off into space, or sing with their eyes continually

closed. The singer with real stage presence conveys meanings directly to the human beings who are listening and gives the impression of being delighted to do so because they are friends.

2. *You appear to be at ease and enjoying what you are doing.* Earlier we called this *poise,* implying qualities of balance and resilience. Being at ease in no way suggests being lazy, sloppy, or disorganized. The ease involved is an assured acceptance of the performer's role as the dominant figure. This lets you feel at home with what you are doing. It imparts an assurance that radiates to the audience as a shared delight in the music and your performance of it.

3. *Your singing focuses attention more on the music than on yourself.* Your technical skills do not call attention to your technique but rather are used to convey the meanings of the music and words. You don't resort to mere physical or vocal gimmickry that makes what you are doing more important than what you are singing. Great actors and actresses make audiences think they *are* the characters they are portraying, because their acting techniques make the qualities of the characters stand out. That is the meaning they want to convey, and their success is measured by how well an audience understands it. In exactly the same way, your effectiveness as a singer is measured by how well your techniques help the audience hear the meanings of the music itself.

4. *You are flexible and not easily rattled.* What if the unexpected happens? What if there is a loud noise outside, the accompanist turns two pages at once and is suddenly way ahead of you, or someone in the audience sneezes loudly in a quiet spot in the music? The performer with real stage presence is not diverted by such things and moreover is able to carry the audience past the incident with an empathetic assurance that says, in effect, "We're not going to be bothered by *that,* are we?"

5. *Your control is continuous.* What you do fills time completely. There are no awkward lapses, no periods when you are "out to lunch," no holes in time during which your audience is expected to look the other way. You are sure of what you are going to do and are able to keep on doing it. You have controlled any nervous mannerisms that work against what you want your audience to see and hear. Your mind "stays in gear." Speakers who burden their delivery with repetitions of "... y'know ..." and "... uh ..." show that they have not mastered this requirement. They will always appear fumbling and uncertain, standing there with their mental motors nervously idling. Singers reveal the same wasteful habits by clearing their throats, assuming tense or awkward postures, fidgeting, and making other small physical signs of underlying nervousness.

CLASS ACTIVITIES

In preparation for the final project outlined in Class Activity 1 of Lesson 34 (p. 139), watch many kinds of television performers: speakers, comedians, singers, actors, panelists. Measure their stage presence against the characteristics listed above. Perhaps you can detect others we missed. Compare and analyze your reactions to performers who catch your interest at once and those who "turn you off." How do these compare with what you want to do in your recital? What did each one do that caused the reaction in you? An interesting variation of this is for all members of the class to watch a specific performance and then bring in individual critiques for class comparison and discussion. If videotape facilities are available, several class members can record their own performances for critique and for comparison with the reports brought in about television performers.

ON YOUR OWN

Write an honest critique of yourself. Don't show it to anyone else. List strengths and weaknesses you think are characteristic of your own performance. Compare these in your mind with the comments made about your work by other class members. Try to specify:

1. Which characteristics of stage presence have you learned to control?

2. Which ones still trouble you? What is the exact reason why that trouble persists? What are you doing or failing to do that accounts for it?

3. What evidences can you find that your singing appears at all artistic to your audience?

APPENDIX 1

Seven Steps to Learning a New Song

Step 1   ***Read the words* ALOUD.**
Make sense: What do the words say? As you read, be sure that you project that meaning, whether the text is poetry or prose. Don't let yourself get trapped in rhymes or sing-song. Read the words more than once, trying each time to use different phrasing, inflections, and meanings. Have someone listen to your reading if you can.

Step 2   ***Tap or clap the rhythm of the melody.***
Study rhythmic notation (pp. 151–54) enough so that you can reproduce the rhythmic patterns of the melody by tapping or clapping them. Get a mental image of how those patterns *sound.*

Step 3   ***Read the words aloud in the rhythms you tapped in Step 2.***
Combine your mental image of the word rhythm with your mental image of the melodic rhythms, creating one composite sound pattern.

Step 4   ***Sing the melody in correct rhythm.***
If you can read notation, sing the melody at sight, combining words, rhythms, and pitches. If you have difficulty doing all three at once, sing the rhythms and pitches first on a neutral syllable, adding the words the second time through. If you cannot yet read notation, have someone play the melody by itself, in strict rhythm and tempo, while you follow it closely. Sing along, the second time through, using the words and rhythms you have already tapped out and spoken.

Step 5   ***Have the accompaniment played while you follow the melody without singing.***
Mentally fit the images of words, rhythms, and melody to the accompaniment. Notice where the accompaniment helps you by playing the melody with the voice part and where it plays something contrasting.

Step 6   ***Sing the melody with the accompaniment.***
Take the lead. Don't wait for the accompaniment to "sing" the melody for you, or even lead you to the next pitch or rhythm. Try to keep your mental image of the melody distinct from what you are expecting the accompaniment to do.

Step 7 *Memorize.*

Repeat the song many times. Gather confidence in singing it, based on your accumulated experiences with the words, rhythms, and melody. Concentrate on the first words of each line as a key to remembering the rest of the line. As soon as you feel some certainty about knowing what comes next without looking at the music, focus your attention on conveying meaning and expression in your singing.

APPENDIX 2

A Sample Vocal Performance Evaluation Form

VOCAL PERFORMANCE EVALUATION

Name _____   Voice _____

Date _____   Evaluator _____

Music performed _____   Composer _____

_____   _____

Instructions: Check the appropriate numbered column for each performance component you feel merits special commendation or needs correction. Assume a rating of 3 for components not checked. Give a summary rating for each principal area, if possible, and add comments and suggestions if time permits.

Rating system:

5 - Excellent. Clearly outstanding in accomplishment or progress.

4 - Good. Substantial accomplishment or progress.

3 - Acceptable. A bare minimum of accomplishment or progress.

2 - Deficient in specific, identifiable ways that outweigh strong points.

1 - Badly faulted. Needs immediate and urgent correction.

Area 1: Use of Voice Component Elements	5	4	3	2	1	Summary rating for Area 1: _____
Posture to support breathing						Comments
Breath control						
Tone quality						
Vowel colors, placement						
Resonance, projection						
Control of registers						
Legato technique						
Area 2: Accuracy Component Elements	5	4	3	2	1	Summary rating for Area 2: _____
Notes						Comments
Rhythms						
Pitch (intonation)						
Dynamics						
Tempos						
Words						
Diction						
Expressive markings						
Area 3: Poise, Expression Component Elements	5	4	3	2	1	Summary rating for Area 3: _____
Poised posture						Comments
Control of mannerisms						
Control of hands						
Facial expressions						
Direct approach to audience						
Phrasing						
Use of mood						
Projection of meaning						

APPENDIX 3

Musicianship Information for Singers

The basic information singers need about how music is organized and written out (notated) is presented here in the following sections:

A. The Score: Staffs and Notation
B. Rhythm: How Music Moves through Time
C. Intervals: The A-B-C's of Melody
D. Scales: Interval Patterns You Know
E. Keys: Tonality and Key Signatures
F. "Road Signs": Tempo, Dynamics, Phrasing, and Expressive Markings

Review Step 7, Lesson 27, regarding the importance of mastering this material.

A. THE SCORE: STAFFS AND NOTATION

Baseball is played on a diamond, which is a formal pattern of specific shape and size, laid out on the ground. Every line, base, and other feature serves a function that is vital to the way the game is played.

The *score* is the musical diamond. Everyone taking part in what goes on there—whether a singer, an instrumentalist, a conductor, or even just a person studying the music—needs to know the meaning of the pattern, its features, and how written music is laid out on it.

The Staff, Tone Letters, and Notes

The most basic feature of this musical diamond is the *staff*, which is a design of lines and spaces that provides room for the notation of all possible tones. Each tone is identified by an alphabet letter from A through G, in a pattern repeated every eight tones in ascending order. The staff representing the entire available range of tones is called the *great staff*:

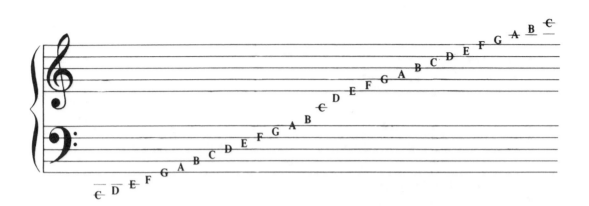

Women's voices normally sing in the upper half of the great staff, identified by the *treble clef sign*, and thus called the *treble staff* or simply the *treble clef*:

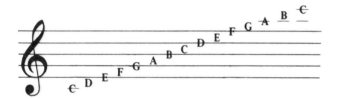

Men's voices normally sing in the lower half of the great staff, identified by the *bass clef sign*, and thus called the *bass staff* or simply the *bass clef*:

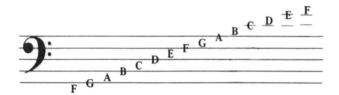

(*Note:* Tenors can also use the treble staff, singing the notes an octave lower.) Learning to recognize and use the letter names of the lines and spaces of the staff you use is the first step in learning to read music. Practice identifying the tones as you sing. Know the letter name of each note you produce. Music, like baseball, is best learned by doing it.

Placement of Notes, Stems, Flags, Bars, and Ledger Lines

Notes representing the pitches (tones) to be sung are placed on the spaces and lines and are identified by the letter name of the space or line on which they are placed. Notes placed on the third line of the staff and above have stems going down from the left side of the note. Notes placed below the third line have stems going up from the right side of the note.

Flags placed on single notes are always on the right of the stem:

Bars replace flags to group notes within the same beat:

Ledger lines add tones above and below the staff:

B. RHYTHM: HOW MUSIC MOVES THROUGH TIME

Music is composed of sound patterns that are measured in time. *Rhythm* is the musical element that explains how this measurement is done and provides notation to write it down. It is probably the easiest musical element to master, because it can be felt physically as patterns of pulses. This suggests that the fastest way to learn it is to *do* it—actually produce the rhythmic sound patterns—rather than merely mastering the theory behind it. "Do the rhythm, then think about it!" is a productive way of thinking. The notation values are listed here, followed by exercises based on the "do it first" approach.

Accurate singing requires that you have security in two principal areas of understanding about rhythm and its notation.

Area 1: Knowledge of Rhythmic Symbols

You need to know note values, meter signatures, bar lines, rests, and use of the dot. Knowing really means being familiar enough with the symbols to be able to use them in doing the rhythm.

Here are the rhythmic notes and symbols the singer needs to know:

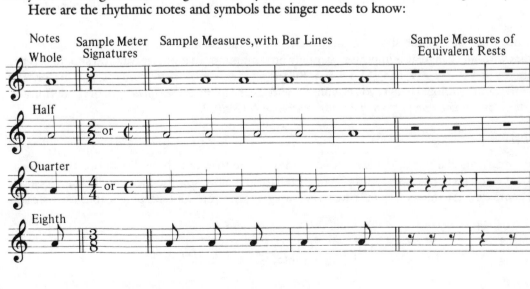

Using the Dot

A dot added to the right of any note lengthens that note by half its value:

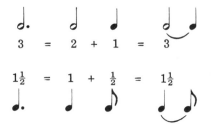

In order to make this concept perfectly clear, make similar equations for all the notes listed above.

Area 2: Understanding Distinctions among Meter, Rhythm, and Tempo

Three terms associated with the subject of rhythm are often confused or used inaccurately. They are *meter, rhythm,* and *tempo.* Real mastery of the rhythmic components of musical performance requires a clear understanding of their exact meanings and of their differences.

Meter

Tap the following pattern with your foot, accenting the first note of each measure as marked. Keep the speed steady, not letting it increase or change in any way.

Notice that you feel the shape of the pattern 1-2-3 immediately; because it is repeated several times without change, it is impressed strongly on your mind. In a similar way you should practice patterns of 1-2, 1-2-3-4, and 1-2-3-4-5-6. By feeling the shape of these patterns, and performing them steadily without change, you can understand the meaning, *by having done it,* of the definition: *Meter is an unchanging pattern of accents, continuously repeated.*

Rhythm

Like many musical terms, *rhythm* is used to mean more than one thing. We defined it earlier as "the measurement of music in time," but there is also a more specific meaning, best understood by comparing it to meter. Tap the pattern below again with your foot, keeping it absolutely steady:

While you go on tapping with your foot, clap with your hands:

$\frac{3}{4}$ | ♪♪ ♪♪ ♪♪ | ♪♪ ♪♪ ♪♪ | ♪♪ ♪♪ ♪♪ |

1 & 2 & 3 &   1 & 2 & 3 &   1 & 2 & 3 & etc.

Together, they look like this:

Hand clapping

Foot tapping

$\frac{3}{4}$

1 & 2 & 3 &   1 & 2 & 3 & etc.

Notice that you can change the hand-clapping pattern without affecting the foot-tapping pattern:

Hand clapping

Foot tapping

$\frac{3}{4}$

1 & 2 & 3 &   1 & 2 & 3 & etc.

In fact, the sky is the limit, for the hand-clapping pattern is completely changeable:

Hand clapping $\frac{3}{4}$

Foot tapping

1 & 2 & 3 &   1 & 2 & 3 &   1 & 2 & 3 & etc.

If you have performed these examples accurately, you can understand the definition: *Rhythm is a changeable pattern of accents, superimposed on the meter.*

Tempo

Here is a familiar song, written with the words (which will represent the melody you already know), the meter (foot tapping), and the rhythm (hand clapping). Sing the melody of the words, tap the meter, and clap the rhythm at the same time.

Words (melody):   My   coun - try,   'tis   of thee, Sweet land of

Clap: $\frac{3}{4}$

Tap:

1   2   3   1   2   3   1   2   3

Words: li - ber-ty,   Of   thee   I   sing!

Clap:

Tap:

1   2   3   1   2   3   1   2   3

When you can do this easily, sing, tap, and clap it faster; then slower. Notice that in both cases the meter remained 1-2-3 and the rhythm bore the same relation to the meter. The only thing that changed was *the rate of speed*. You have now learned, by doing, the definition: *Tempo means only the rate of speed and does not affect meter or rhythm.*

Suggested Activities for Further Practice in Rhythm

1. Practice a thoroughly familiar song in the following ways:
    a. Tap the meter with your foot, using the meter called for by the meter signature.
    b. Clap the rhythm of the melody with your hands while you tap the meter with your foot.
    c. Sing the melody while you tap and clap.

2. Using a completely unfamiliar song, read the meter (by tapping with your foot) and the rhythm of the melody (by hand clapping). Use a slow tempo to begin with, speeding it slightly the second and third times through. Identify what you find hard to do. Work with your instructor and other class members for mutual assistance.

3. Tap the meter of music you hear on radio or recordings. Identify the metric pattern as 1-2, 1-2-3, or 1-2-3-4. Clap the rhythm of the melody at the same time, if you can, without changing the metric pattern that you are tapping.

C. INTERVALS: THE A-B-C's OF MELODY

What does an alphabet letter mean? Well, anything, or nothing, or many things, depending on how it is used. As a child you might have asked such a question, but now you know so many answers you don't think about it. You simply recognize the letter as a part of the fabric of language, and you use it.

Intervals are the alphabet letters of music. What do they mean? Technically an interval is the distance between two tones, but that has meaning only when you experience the sound of that distance. It takes time to learn all the possible intervals this way, but the effort brings the considerable reward of more precise, musical singing.

A melody uses intervals in two ways. First, the melody itself is a succession of intervals arranged in a rhythmic pattern. Secondly, the melody is based on a supporting harmony, which is composed of groups of intervals played simultaneously. Knowing and being able to produce correct intervals in your singing is thus of primary importance to accurate performance of melodies. Here are four workable premises on which to begin a systematic study of intervals:

1. *Intervals are best understood by sound and not merely by theory.* To say that an interval is the distance between tones doesn't help you sing it; you must *hear* that distance as actual sound. Here is an interval called a fifth; that is, there are five scale steps between the tones:

The term *fifth* remains only a technical description until you sing:

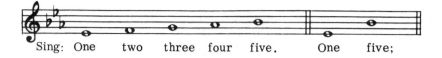
Sing: One two three four five. One five;

Just producing and hearing the sounds identifies the concept of a fifth in ways no words can. Conclusion: *TO KNOW AN INTERVAL, SING IT.*

2. *You already know the sound of several basic intervals.* If you have sung a popular song, folksong, hymn—*any* melody—you have used the most common intervals, since melody is simply a succession of intervals. This means that you probably know—that is, can recognize—such intervals as the octave, the second, the fifth, and the third, just because you have reproduced their sounds in singing, even though you did not identify them by name.

3. *The next step is to relate what you know to the symbols for those sounds.* When you can associate what your ear already understands with the visual symbols that represent it, you have begun music reading. It is an association that flows two ways; knowing what the sound is strengthens your ability to recognize the symbol, and seeing the symbol will trigger your mental image of the sound.

4. *Seeing notation will tell you what exact sounds to sing.* Trust the process. Develop the habit of looking at notation closely, *expecting* it to give you the information you need. This will lessen your dependence on getting it by ear from someone else's singing or playing. You can count on notation to work for you if:

    a.   You look at it closely;

    b.   You always apply everything you have learned about it;

    c.   You pay persistent, continuous attention to it.

Learning Interval Sizes

The following information about interval sizes and sounds refers specifically to what a *singer* needs to know, as contrasted with the knowledge needed to play the piano or other instrument or to compose music. In order to sing an interval you have to form a mental image of it; then you can produce it. To establish such images in your mind takes practice and repetition; singing the following examples will be a good beginning.

1. *How to measure the* overall *size of an interval.* Intervals are identified by numbers indicating their size, or the distance between the two notes involved. The general, or overall, size can be seen at a glance by calling one note "one" and counting every line and space to the other note, either up or down. The number falling on the second note names the overall size of the interval.

    Interval: 5th   Interval: 6th

Here are intervals measured up from middle C, named by their overall sizes. Remember that interval size can be measured from any tone to any other tone, in either direction. Notice that each interval is written in two ways: *melodically* (one note following another), and *harmonically* (at the same time).

    2nd   3rd   4th   5th   6th   7th   Octave (8th)   9th

2. *How to measure the* exact *size of an interval.* Most of these intervals have more than one size, and accurate singing demands that you be able to distinguish between the overall size and the exact size. These differences of size actually produce different intervals, such as a major third and a minor third, even though they use the same overall size name, the third. The most completely accurate method of measuring exact interval sizes is to find out how many minor 2nds, or *half steps* (the smallest possible interval) are contained in the interval being measured. Here are all the intervals in an octave, with the number of half steps in each.

You can also use the keyboard as a visual guide to the number of half steps in the intervals. Here is a graphic representation of the octave between C and C. The circled numbers on each key tell the number of half steps between that tone and the lower C. You can also reverse the process and count half steps down from the upper C. Drill at a keyboard is very useful; simply by playing the tones of an interval both melodically and harmonically, you can check its exact sound as you are trying to memorize it.

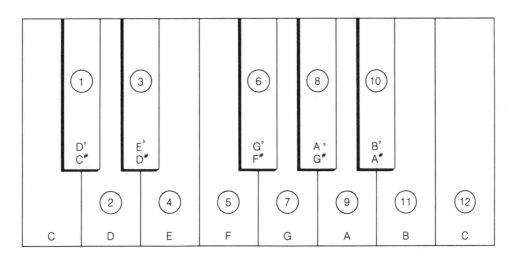

Suggested Activities for Further Practice with Intervals

1.   Above and between the notes of the melody line of a familiar song, write the overall size of every interval. When they are all written, sing the melody. Concentrate on hearing each interval size as you sing it, relying as little as possible on your familiarity with the whole melody. For this exercise to be of maximum benefit in helping you learn and recognize intervals, you need to hear each one as a separate unit.

2.   Apply the procedure of Activity 1 to an unfamiliar melody. As you try to sing the intervals you wrote down, don't give up too quickly. You will be learning the melody by letting the note symbols trigger the sounds of the intervals in your mind.

3.   Practice singing specific intervals. Choose a tone at random, and sing octaves, 5ths, 4ths, and 3rds both up and down from it. This is most effective if you work with other people, since you can then help and correct each other. Have someone who plays the piano play the interval *after* you have tried to sing it.

D. SCALES: INTERVAL PATTERNS YOU KNOW

Scales are fixed patterns of intervals. They are organized around specific starting tones, called *key tones,* and they extend up or down to the next tone of the same letter name. A scale pattern may start on any tone. Your ear is already very familiar with the pattern called the *major scale,* and it probably also recognizes some forms of the *minor scale,* simply because virtually all the music you have ever heard uses those patterns.

The Major Scale Pattern

Scale patterns are composed of half steps (½) and whole steps (1), and it is the order of those steps within the pattern that gives the scale its unique sound and identity. For example, the major scale pattern (the one you know best) is: 1 - 1 - ½ - 1 - 1 - 1 - ½. In notation, starting on middle C, this is written:

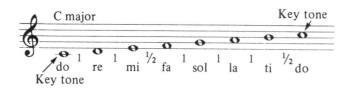

When you play this scale (C major) on the keyboard, you will notice that it uses only the white keys, leaving out the black keys. This shows that the scale pattern is selective, since it uses some tones and omits others. Major scales starting on other tones would use some black keys and omit some white keys; the pattern of half and whole steps given above, however, remains the same for any major scale. Notice how familiar this pattern is to you, regardless of where you start it, just because so many of the songs you know use it.

A little study shows that the major scale includes all possible intervals between its various tones. You can check this at the keyboard and by starting with a scale tone and finding another scale tone that is the right number of half steps away, as in the following example:

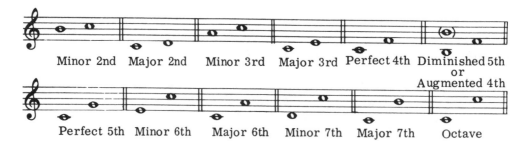

The Minor Scale Patterns

By changing the pattern to include some of the notes omitted by the major scale, *minor scales* are created. With the major, these complete the list of commonly used scales. Like the major, they are simply patterns of intervals organized around a central tone. They are probably best understood by relating them to the major scale pattern. The singer needs to be familiar with the three forms of minor scale in ordinary use.

The *natural minor* lowers the 3rd, 6th, and 7th tones of the major scale by one half step. This is written by inserting the correct *accidental sign* (in this case either a flat or a natural) before the note:

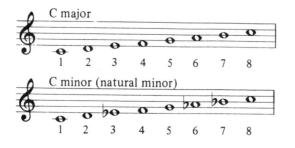

The *harmonic minor* lowers the 3rd and 6th tones, but leaves the 7th tone in its natural position. Notice that this produces an interval of three half steps in the scale between tones 6 and 7; it is called an *augmented 2nd* and gives this scale a unique sound.

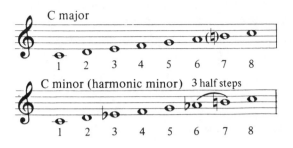

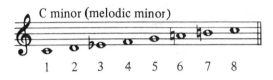

The *melodic minor* combines the first two forms. Singing up the scale you use this pattern:

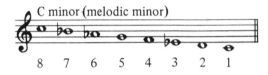

Singing down the scale you use:

C minor (melodic minor)

While detailed understanding of minor scales and other possible scale patterns such as modes must properly be left to the study of music theory, singers need to be able to recognize the minor pattern when it occurs in their melody lines and use its notation accurately in singing those lines. Since the minor mode is usually thought to have different expressive qualities from the major, confusing the two creates serious mistakes, both in the wrong notes that are sung and in the distorted expression that is given to the music. A comic example can be heard simply by playing the melody of the *Wedding March* from Wagner's *Tannhäuser* in minor.

E. KEYS: TONALITY AND KEY SIGNATURES

The idea of a musical key can be related to the analogy of the baseball diamond. One tone—the *key tone*—is heard as the dominating tone in a group of related tones (the scale pattern), just as home plate is the most important of the four bases. Like home plate, the key tone is the one you start from and return to (in the scale pattern) to achieve a feeling of completion. Any tone can serve as a key tone if you then select the right tones to go with it to make the correct scale pattern. This involves changing certain tones by the use of accidentals: a *sharp* (#) to raise the pitch a half step and a *flat* (♭) to lower it a half step. The whole group of tones—the key tone and the scale pattern—makes up the *key*. The sections that follow list the accidentals that must be inserted to produce major scale patterns starting on all tones other than C.

Keys Requiring Sharps

To start a major scale on the tone G, we must alter one of the notes of the C scale (F) by sharping it, so that the size of each interval in the scale going up from G corresponds to the major scale pattern: 1 - 1 - ½ - 1 - 1 - 1 - ½.

G major

1   1 $\frac{1}{2}$ 1   1   1 $\frac{1}{2}$

In a similar way, scales built on the following tones call for sharps:

Starting the major scale on:	Requires that sharps be added to:
D	F and C
A	F, C, and G
E	F, C, G, and D
B	F, C, G, D, and A
F#	F, C, G, D, A, and E

Keys Requiring Flats

To start a major scale on the tone F, we must add a flat to the tone B to create the major scale pattern of intervals:

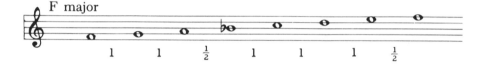

F major

1   1 $\frac{1}{2}$ 1   1   1 $\frac{1}{2}$

Similarly, scales built on the following tones call for the addition of flats:

Starting the major scale on:	Requires that flats be added to:
B♭	B and E
E♭	B, E, and A
A♭	B, E, A, and D
D♭	B, E, A, D, and G
G♭	B, E, A, D, G, and C

There are twenty-six keys used in music: thirteen major and thirteen minor. These are identified by *key signatures,* which are combinations of symbols at the beginning of each line of music, showing what accidentals are needed to make the scale pattern come out right when starting from the key tone of that piece.

Since you are a singer, the principal thing you need to obtain from the key signature is the location of the key tone, because that tells you where to start the scale pattern you hear in your mind. In terms of the baseball analogy, if you can see where home plate (the key tone) is you can go to bat; you already know the rest of the diamond (your mental ear hears the scale pattern).

Identifying Keys in Sharps

If the signature is in sharps, the key tone for major keys is found on the line or space immediately above the last sharp to the right in the signature; for minor keys, it is on the line or space immediately below the last sharp to the right.

Key of D major   Key of F-sharp minor

Identifying Keys in Flats

If the signature is in flats, the key tone for major keys is found three steps (line, space, line; or space, line, space) below the last flat to the right in the signature; for minor keys, it is two steps above the last flat to the right.

Key of A-flat major   Key of B-flat minor

Chart of Key Signatures

Here are all the commonly used key signatures. Notice that each one stands for both a major and a minor key and that key tones are given for both. Since both are related to the same signature, when you are in the major key you refer to the other as the *relative minor,* and vice versa. Remember, the key tone is where the scale pattern starts.

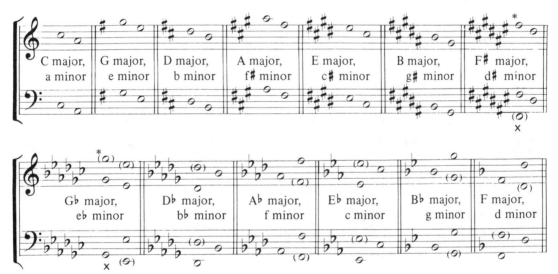

* same key and pitch on the piano
x

Suggested Activities for Further Practice with Keys and Scales

1. Review the songs you have worked on for this class. Identify the key signature and key tone for each. With the instructor's help, determine whether the song is in major or minor. This assignment may be expanded to every song in the Song Collection.

2. In any music book you can find, practice identifying key signatures at sight. Use the methods given above, but try to develop the ability to identify the key at a glance.

F. "ROAD SIGNS": TEMPO, DYNAMICS, PHRASING, AND EXPRESSIVE MARKINGS

You would feel foolish if you drove up to a highway bridge that was washed out and had a workman tell you that you passed a "Road Closed" sign about three miles back without noticing it. "It's a real plain sign!" he adds, helpfully. It might ease some of your frustration to get angry, but it wouldn't get you any closer to your destination. "Next time," you might tell yourself, "I'll remember to read the road signs."

In music it is easy to pass up "road signs" posted for your guidance and then wonder why your singing doesn't sound as expressive or accurate as you hoped it would. If the composer puts in a sign reading "*Con amore, espressivo, decrescendo al pianissimo*," and you just pass by it because you're not looking or you don't understand all that Italian, you will run off the road the composer had laid out, and you won't be quite sure why. Your singing won't convey the expression he or she had in mind, which the sign said was to be done "Tenderly, with expression, fading out to very soft."

Every marking in a good score tells you something specific to do. Each one is intended to modify the sound of your performance. You realize that this is true of notes, rhythms, the staff, clefs, and so on. It is equally true—and important—of such directions as *ritard, crescendo, allegro, D.C.,* and *sfz.* Each one is put there to influence your sound. This can happen only if you read the sign.

The sections that follow list three groups of signs that you should look for and learn to use. To make them effective in your singing, train yourself to do three things:

1. *Look at every sign*. There might be one telling you to stop and wait. (Well, there actually *is*: G.P. means "general pause.")

2. *If you don't know what it means, find out*. Look it up. Ask someone. Examine how it applies to the music you are singing. Write the meaning in your score.

3. *Use it*. Make it *happen* in the way you sing the music. Then remember it!

Group 1: Tempo Markings

Terms for Specific Rates of Speed

Prestissimo	(quickest)	
Presto	(quick)	Very fast
Vivace	(lively)	
Allegro		
Con moto	(with motion)	Fast
Allegro con moto		
Allegretto	(a little fast)	Moderately fast
Moderato		
Andante	(walking speed)	Moderately
Adagio	(at ease)	
Larghetto	(a little broadly)	Moderately slow
Largo	(broadly)	
Lento		Slowly

Terms for Changing the Rate of Speed

Accelerando	Get faster
Stringendo	Faster, more excited
Ritard (rit.)	
Ritardando	Get slower
Rallentando (rall.)	
Rubato	Freely changing tempo

Group 2: Dynamic Markings

Markings for Fixed Dynamic Levels

pp, pianissimo   Softest controllable tone

p, piano   Softly

mp, mezzo piano   Moderately soft

mf, mezzo forte   Moderately loud

f, forte   Loudly

ff, fortissimo   Loudest controllable tone

Markings for Changing Dynamic Levels

Cresc., crescendo

                                                  Get louder

Subito f (suddenly loud)

Dim., diminuendo, decrescendo

                                                  Get softer

Subito p (suddenly soft)

Morendo   Die away

Sfz, sffz, sforzando   Accents; suddenly louder; percussive tones

Group 3: Markings for Phrasing and Expression

⌢ (*fermata*)   Hold the note at least twice its length

, (breathing mark)   Break the melody line to breathe

                                       Sing all the notes under the line in one syllable
                                       or breath or as a single thought

//   Break the flow of the line completely

‖: :‖   Repeat everything between these markings

𝄋 (*segno*, sign)   Repeat from (*dal segno*) or to (*al segno*) the
                                       place marked by this sign

Agitato   Agitated, excited

Animato   Animated, with spirit

Appassionato   Intensely, with great emotion

Assai   Much, as in *Allegro assai* (very fast)

Colla voce (with the voice)   Usually a designation that the accompaniment
                                       is to follow the singer

Con amore (with love)	Tenderly, with deep emotion
Con espressione (con espr.), espressivo	With expression or emotional coloring
D.C. *(Da capo)*	Return to the beginning (the "head") of the piece and sing again to the end or to the word *Fine* if given
D.S. *(Dal segno)*	Return to the sign (*𝄋*) and sing again to the end or to the word *Fine* if given
Devotamente	Devoutly, with religious feeling
Dolce	Sweetly
Fine	End, finish; indicates where a piece concludes if only part of it has been repeated
G.P.	General pause
Grazioso	Gracefully, graciously, gently
Ma non troppo	"But not too much," as in *Allegro ma non troppo* ("fast, but not too fast," or "don't rush!")
Molto	A lot, a great deal, as in *crescendo molto* (a big crescendo; much louder)
Poco a poco	Little by little
Smorzando, morendo	Fading away, dying out
Tranquillo	Calmly, tranquilly

If your music contains a marking not listed here, remember what you were urged to do above in such a case: *Look it up!* (Most music dictionaries will be able to help you.)

Suggested Activities for Further Practice with Signs

Go through the music of a familiar song, circling in red pencil every marking listed here that you can find. Then sing the song for the class, taking special care to see each sign and do exactly what it says. Class critiques can be held on individual performances. The same procedure can be applied to a completely unfamiliar song or one you have just started to work on. Compare this to driving down an unfamiliar road: You are careful to watch the road itself (the notes, words, and rhythms), but, since you are not familiar with the territory, you are also careful to look for road signs. See how well you can do it.

Concert Songs

O REST IN THE LORD

Felix Mendelssohn
From Elijah

sires; ___ O rest __ in the Lord, wait pa‑tient‑ly for

Him, and He __ shall __ give thee thy heart's __ de —

sires, _____ and He shall give thee thy heart's de‑

sires. Com‑mit thy way un‑to Him, and trust in

Him; com-mit thy way un - to Him, and trust in

cresc.

Him; and fret __ not thy - self _____ be-cause of e - vil

p

do - ers. O rest in the Lord, wait pa - tient-ly for

Him, wait pa-tient-ly for Him; O rest in the

Lord, wait pa-tient-ly for Him, and He shall ___

give thee thy heart's ___ de - sires, ___ and He shall

give ___ thee thy heart's de - sires, and He shall

give ___ thee thy heart's de - sires. O rest in the

Lord, O rest in the Lord, and wait, ———— wait ——

pa - tient- ly for Him.

AWAKE, SWEET LOVE

High key

John Dowland
First Book of Ayres, 1597
Adapted by Royal Stanton

A-wake, sweet love, thou art re-turned! My heart, which long in ab - sence mourned, lives now in per-fect joy. ___ Let love, which nev - er ab - sent dies, Now live for - ev - er in her/his eyes, whence came my first an - noy. ___

On-ly her-self hath seem-ed fair; She on-ly I could love;
him-self He

She on-ly drove me to des-pair, when she un-kind did prove;
He he

Des-pair did make me wish to die, that I my joys might end;

rit.

She on-ly who did make me fly, my state may now a - mend.
He

rit.

AWAKE, SWEET LOVE

Low key

John Dowland
First Book of Ayres, 1597
Adapted by Royal Stanton

A-wake, sweet love, thou art re-turned! My heart, which long in ab - sence

mourned, lives now in per - fect joy._____ Let love, which nev - er

ab - sent dies, Now live for - ev - er in her eyes, / his eyes, whence came my first an-

noy._____ On-ly her - self / him - self hath seem - ed fair; She / He on-ly I could love;

She / He on-ly drove me to des - pair, when she / he un - kind did prove;

Des-pair did make me wish to die, that I my joys might end;

She / He on-ly who did make me fly, my state may now a - mend.

rit.

MODEL OF A MODERN MAJOR-GENERAL

Arthur Sullivan
From Pirates of Penzance
Edited by Royal Stanton

Allegro vivace (as fast as the diction can be made clear)

I am the ver-y mod-el of a mod-ern Ma-jor Gen-er-al; I've in-for-ma-tion veg-e-ta-ble, an-i-mal, and min-er-al; I know the kings of Eng-land and I quote the fights his-tor-i-cal, From

Mar - a - thon to Wat-er-loo, in   or-der cat - e - gor - i - cal; I'm   ver - y well ac-quaint - ed, too, with

mat - ters math - e - mat - i - cal, I   un-der-stand e - qua-tions, both the sim-ple and quad-rat-i-cal; A-

(Pauses, at a loss for a rhyme)

bout bi - no - mial the - o - rem I'm teem-ing with a   lot o' news,   With

man-y cheer - ful facts a-bout the square of the hy-pot-e-nuse!   I'm

very good at in-te-gral and dif-fer-ren-tial cal-cu-lus; I know the sci-en-tif-ic names of

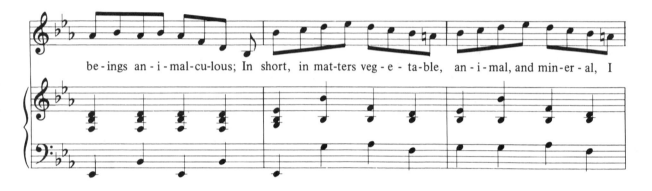

be-ings an-i-mal-cu-lous; In short, in mat-ters veg-e-ta-ble, an-i-mal, and min-er-al, I

am the ver-y mod-el of a mod-ern Ma-jor Gen-er-al!

BEAU SOIR

English translation
by Royal Stanton

Claude Debussy

Andante, ma non troppo

When in the set-ting sun flow-ing wa-ters are shin - ing;
Lorsque au sol-eil cou - chant les ri - viè - res sont ro - ses,

When a shim - mer-ing light lies on the roll - ing plain,
Et qu'un tié - de fris - son court sur les champs de blé,

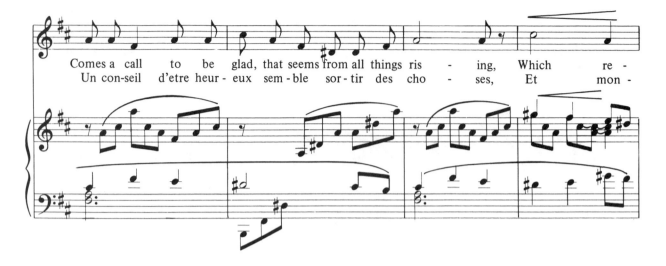

Comes a call to be glad, that seems from all things ris - ing, Which re -
Un con-seil d'etre heur - eux sem - ble sor - tir des cho - ses, Et mon -

poco rit.   *a tempo*   **p**

sounds in my heart___ in pain.   For it
ter vers le coeur___ trou - blé.   Un con-

poco rit.   *a tempo*

animando e cresc.

calls me to taste the full - est joy of be - ing, in this hour of my
seil de goû - ter le char - me d'être au mon - de, Ce-pen-dant qu'on est

youth, while eve-nings still are fair; _____ For we must all de-
jeune et que le soir est beau, _____ Car nous nous en al-

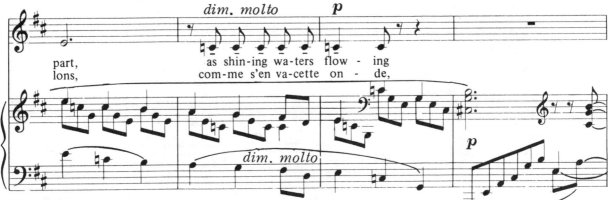

part,   as shin-ing wa-ters flow - ing
lons,   com-me s'en va-cette on - de,

Move   to the sea,
Elle   à la mer,

We   to   the   tomb. _____
nous   au   tom - beau. _____

BID ME TO LIVE

Robert Herrick
(altered)

Royal Stanton

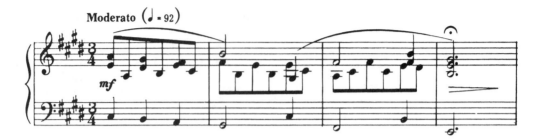

1. Bid me to live, and I will live
2. Thou art my life, my love, my heart;

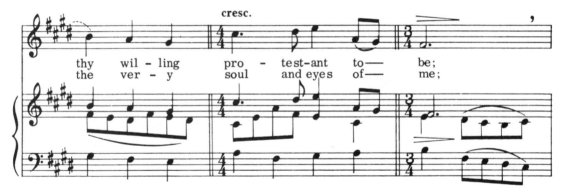

thy wil – ling pro – test-ant to —— be;
the ver – y soul and eyes of —— me;

Or bid me love —— and I —— will
Thou hast com – mand —— of ev —— 'ry

give a lov-ing heart —— to —— thee, a heart as sound and
part, to live and die —— for —— thee, to live and die for

free, a heart as soft and kind as in the
thee, so bid me die that I may dare the cold

whole world thou canst find; That heart I'll give, that
death to come to me, Or bid me live, that thy

heart —— I'll give to thee! ————
pro —— test - ant to be! ————

CARO MIO BEN

High key

Giuseppe Giordani

Dear one, be-lieve, when we must part, I can but grieve deep in my
Ca - ro mio ben, cre - di - mi al-men, sen - za di te lan - gui-sce il

heart.___ Dear one, be-lieve, I can but grieve deep in ___ my
cor,___ ca - ro mio ben, sen - za di te___ lan - gui - sce il

heart. Faith - ful to thee I'll ev - er
cor. Il tuo fe - del so - spi-ra o-

be; Why must thou be__ so__ cruel to__ me? Why must thou be So cruel to
gnor. Ces - sa, cru - del, tan - to ri - gor! Ces - sa, cru - del, tan - to ri -

me?__ So cruel to me? Dear one, be-lieve, when we must part, I can but
gor,__ tan - to ri - gor! Ca - ro mio ben, cre - di mi al-men, sen - za di

grieve deep in__ my heart; Dear one, be-lieve, I can but grieve, When we must
te - lan - gui - sce il cor, ca - ro mio ben, cre - di mi al-men, sen - za di

part,__ Deep in my heart.
te__ lan - gui - sce il cor.

CARO MIO BEN

Low key

Giuseppe Giordani

Larghetto (♩ = 60)

Dear one, be-lieve, when we must part, I can but grieve deep_ in my heart._
Ca - ro mio ben, cre - di - mi al-men, sen - za di te lan - gui - sce il cor,_

Dear one, be-lieve, I can but grieve deep_ in__ my heart._
ca - ro mio ben, sen - za di te lan - gui - sce il cor._

Faith - ful to thee I'll ev - er
Il tuo fe - del so - spi - ra o-

be; Why must thou be so cruel to me? Why must thou be So cruel to
gnor. Ces - sa, cru - del, tan - to ri - gor! Ces - sa, cru - del, tan - to ri -

me?— So cruel to me?— Dear one, be - lieve, When we must part, I can but
gor,— tan - to ri - gor! Ca - ro mio ben, cre - di mi al - men, sen - za di

grieve deep in my heart; Dear one, be - lieve, I can but grieve, When we must
te lan - gui - sce il cor, ca - ro mio ben, cre - di mi al - men, sen - za di

part,— Deep in my heart.
te lan - gui - sce il cor.

COME AGAIN! SWEET LOVE

High key

John Dowland
Accompaniment by Royal Stanton

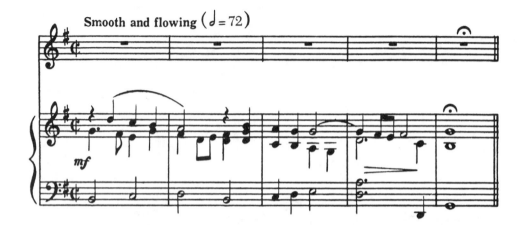

Smooth and flowing ($\mathd = 72$)

1. Come a - gain!　　　Sweet　love　doth
2. Come a - gain!　　　That　I　may
3. All the day　　　the　sun　that

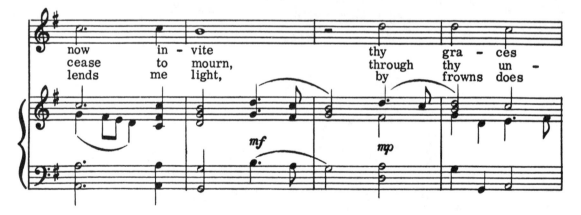

now　　in - vite　　thy　gra - ces
cease　　to　mourn,　through　thy　un -
lends　me　light,　by　thy　frowns　does

that re -   frain   To   do   me
kind dis - dain,   For   now,   left
cause me   pain,   And   feeds me

due   de - light;   To   see,   to hear,
all   for - lorn,   I   sit,   I sigh,
with   de - lay.   Her smiles, my springs

to touch,   to kiss,   to die, ——————
I weep,   I faint,   I die, ——————
that make   my joys   to grow, ——————

with thee a - gain   in   sweet est sym – – pa - thy!
in dead - ly pain   and end - less mis – – er - y!
her frowns that win   in   sweet est sym – – pa - thy!

COME AGAIN! SWEET LOVE

Low key

John Dowland
Accompaniment by Royal Stanton

1. Come a - gain! Sweet love doth now in - to
2. Come a - gain! That I may cease to
3. All the day the sun that lends me

vite thy gra - ces that re - frain
mourn, through thy un - kind dis - dain,
light, by frowns does cause me pain,

DEDICATION (Widmung)

Robert Franz
Edited by Royal Stanton

Thine are the songs thou hear'st me sing - ing; I found___ them
Dein sind sie al - le ja ge - we - sen, aus dein - er

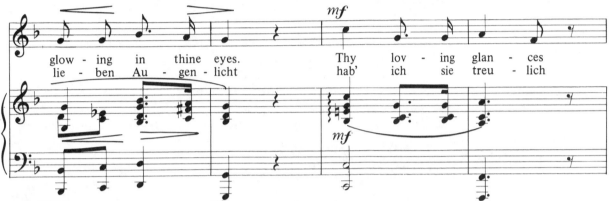

glow - ing in thine eyes. Thy lov - ing glan - ces
lie - ben Au - gen - licht hab' ich sie treu - lich

helped___ me read them. Dost thou not know___ they are___ thine
ab - ge - le - sen, kennst du die eig - nen Lie - der

own? Dost thou not know___ they are___ thine own?
nicht? Kennst du die eig - nen Lie - der nicht?

DEDICATION *(Zueignung)*

German text by Hermann von Gilm
English words by Royal Stanton

Richard Strauss

For the love you send to cheer me When I can - not
Ja, du weisst es, teu - re See - le, dass ich fern von

have you near me, Love to bind us when a - part,
dir— mich quä - le, Lie - be macht die Her - zen krank,

Thanks, dear heart!
ha - be Dank.

For   the joy   that der   Love   has brought   me,
Einst   hielt ich,   that der   Frei — heit Ze — cher,

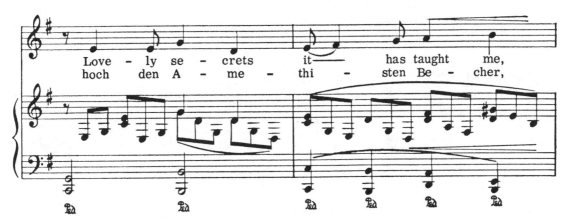

Love — ly se — crets   it — has taught   me,
hoch   den A — me — thi — sten Be — cher,

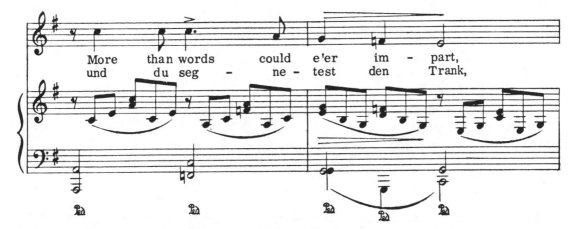

More   than words   could e'er im — part,
und   du seg — ne — test den   Trank,

Thanks, dear heart!
ha — be Dank.

con espr.

MY DESPAIR *(Star Vicino)*

Low key
English words
by Royal Stanton

Salvatore Rosa

is to —— know,—— to —— know —— you're near – by!　　　To
go di – let – to, di – let – to d'a—— mor,　　　Più

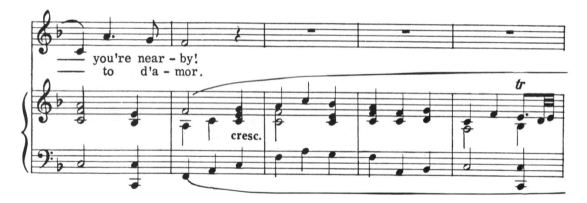

know ———— you're　near – by,————
va ———— go di – let'————

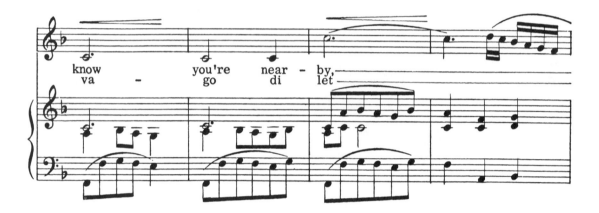

—— you're near – by!
—— to　d'a - mor.

cresc.

tr

My love　laughs in　the　joy　of　your
Star lon - tan　da　co - lei　che　si

dim.

dolce

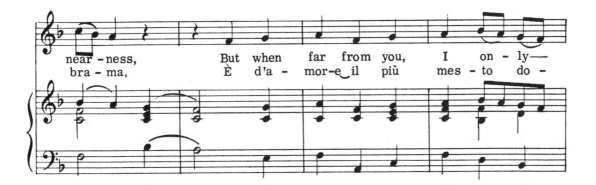

near-ness, But when far from you, I on - ly —
bra - ma, È d'a - mor-e il più mes - to do -

cry, — But when far, But when far,
lor! — È d'a - mor-e il più mes —

— But when — far from you— I — on-ly cry! When far
— to do - lor, è il più, mes-to do - lor, più mes -

from you, I on - ly cry!
to do - lor, — il più — mes-to do - lor!

rit.

MY DESPAIR *(Star Vicino)*

High key
English words
by Royal Stanton

Salvatore Rosa

you're near-by!
to   d'a-mor.

My love
Star lon-

laughs in the joy of your near-ness,   But when far from you, I on-ly___ cry,___
tan da co - lei che si bra-ma,   È d'a-mor-è il più mes-to do - lor!___

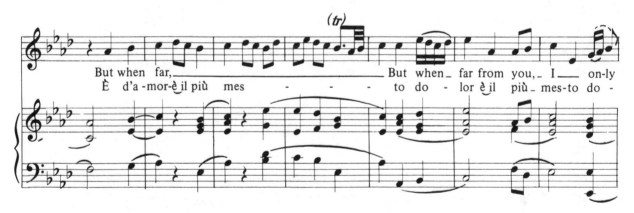

But when far,_____ But when_ far from you,_ I___ on-ly
È d'a-mor-è il più mes -   -   - to do - lor è il più_ mes-to do-

cry! When far   from   you I_____ on-ly cry!
lor, più mes - to   do - lor_____ il più__ mes-to do-lor!

FOREVER BLESSED

High key

G. F. Handel
Adapted from Jephtha
by Royal Stanton

Forever bless-ed be Thy ho-ly name,
Lord God of Is - ra-el! Lord God of Is - ra-
el; For - ev-er, For - ev-er bless-ed be Thy ho-ly
name, for-ev-er, for-ev-er bless - ed be___ Thy ho-ly name,___

Lord God of Is - ra - el, Lord God of Is - ra - el! _____ For -

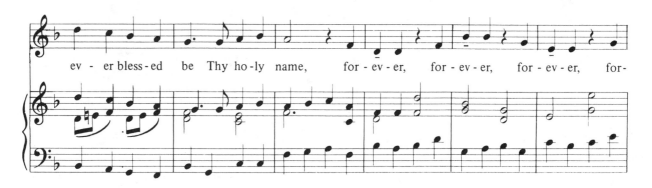

ev - er bless - ed be Thy ho - ly name, for - ev - er, for - ev - er, for - ev - er, for-

ev - er, for - ev - er, for - ev - er ____ Blest be Thy ho - ly name, for - ev - er

blest Thy name, Lord God of Is - ra - el!

FOREVER BLESSED

Low key

G. F. Handel
Adapted from Jephtha
by Royal Stanton

Lord God of Is - ra - el, Lord God of Is - ra - el! _____ For

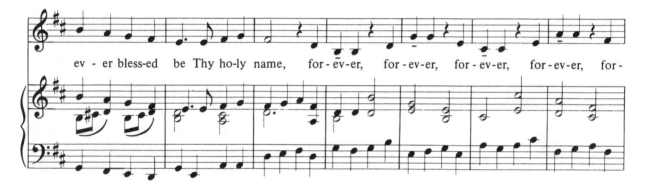

ev - er bless-ed be Thy ho-ly name, for-ev-er, for-ev-er, for-ev-er, for-ev-er, for-

ev - er, for - ev - er _____ Blest be Thy ho - ly name, for-ev - er blest Thy

name, Lord God of Is - ra - el!

GRANT ME THIS FAVOR

G. F. Handel
From Theodora

Grant me this favor, dear-est one: Make me your

faith-ful guard. Grant me this

fav-or dear-est one: Make me your faith-ful guard, To

shield you from bleak wind—— and storm, A smile,   a

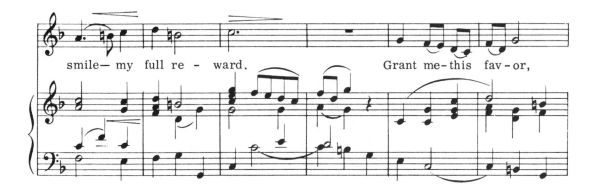

smile— my full re - ward.   Grant me-this fav-or,

make me your faith-ful   guard;   Dear— est one!

Dear— est one!   Make me your faith-ful,   faith—ful guard;

A smile, a smile, A

smile my full re - ward! Make me your faith - ful, faith-ful

guard! To shield you from bleak wind and storm

A smile,

a smile —————— my-full re-ward! Make me your

faith - ful guard, to shield you from bleak wind and storm, ————

A smile, a

rit.

smile —— my full —— re-ward!

colla voce   a tempo   *mp*

rit.

I ATTEMPT FROM LOVE'S SICKNESS TO FLY

Henry Purcell

In moderate time, with expression — rit. — a tempo

I at-tempt from Love's

sick-ness to fly___ in_ vain,_ Since I am, my-

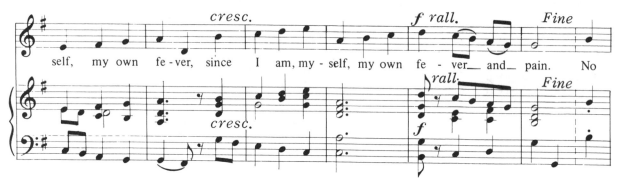

self, my own fe-ver, since I am, my-self, my own fe-ver_ and_ pain. No

more now, no more now, fond_ heart, with pride should we swell, Thou canst not_ raise_

forces, thou canst not raise for-ces e - nough to re - bel! I at-tempt from Love's

sick-ness to fly_____ in_ vain,- Since I am, my - self, my own fe-ver, since

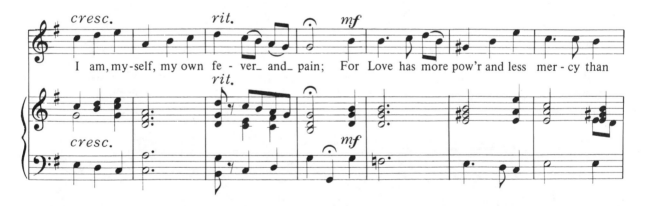

I am, my-self, my own fe - ver_ and_ pain; For Love has more pow'r and less mer-cy than

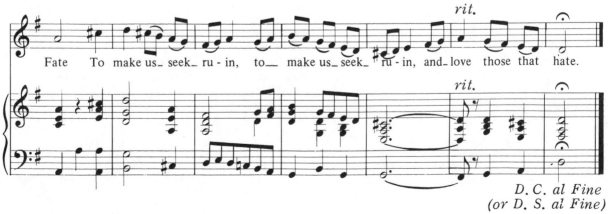

Fate To make us_ seek_ ru - in, to_ make us_ seek_ ru - in, and_ love those that hate.

D. C. al Fine
(or D. S. al Fine)

LITANY *(Litanei)*

High key
English words
by Royal Stanton

Franz Schubert

Lento devotamente (♪ = 72)

1. Lord, with thank-ful heart____ I praise____ Thee,
2. When the care of life____ dis-mays____ me,
1. Ruh'n in Frie - den al - le See - len,
2. Und die nie - der Son - ne lach - ten,

Who to loft - ier aims doth raise me, For the joy Thy love_be-stows,
And my fee - ble will be-trays me,Then Thy love my zeal_re-stores,
die voll-bracht ein bang - es Quäl-en die vol-len-det sü - ssenTraum,
un - termMond auf Dor - nen wach-ten,Gott,im rein-en Him-mels-licht,

And the peace that from it flows, Strength and com - fort ev - er_ giv - ing,
Cour - age new in - to me pours, All my bright - est hope re - new - ing,
le - bens - satt ge - bo - ren Kaum, aus der Welt hin - ü - ber schei - den;
einst zu seh'n von An - ge - sicht: Al - le, die von hin - nen_ schei - den;

rit.

a tempo

Lord, with thank - ful heart_____ I praise_____ Thee!
Lord, with thank - ful heart_____ I praise_____ Thee!
Al - le See - len ruh'n_____ in Frie - den!
Al - le See - len ruh'n_____ in Frie - den!

pp

LITANY *(Litanei)*

Low key
English words
by Royal Stanton

Franz Schubert

Lento devotamente (♪ = 72)

1. Lord, with thank-ful heart____ I praise_Thee,
2. When the care of life____ dis-mays_ me,
1. Ruh'n in Frie - den al - le See - len,
2. Und die nie-der Son - ne lach - ten,

Who to loft - ier aims____ doth raise me, For the joy Thy love_be-stows,_
And my fee - ble will____ be - trays me, Then Thy love my zeal_re-stores,_
die voll-bracht ein bang - es Quä-len, die vol-len-det süs -sen Traum,_
un - term Mond auf Dor - nen wach-ten, Gott, im rei-nen Him-mels-licht,_

And the peace that from it flows, Strength and com - fort ev - er___ giv - ing,
Cour - age new in - to me pours, All my bright - est hope re - new - ing,
le - bens-satt, ge - bo - ren kaum, aus der Welt hin - ü - ber schei-den;
einst zu seh'n von An - ge-sicht: Al - le, die von hin-nen schei-den;

Lord, with thank - ful heart_____ I praise_____ Thee!
Lord, with thank - ful heart_____ I praise_____ Thee!
Al - le See - len ruh'n_____ in Frie - den!
Al - le See - len ruh'n_____ in Frie - den!

LORD, TO THEE

G. F. Handel

Lord, to—thee, each night and day,

strong in hope we sing and—pray.

Strong in hope we sing ____ and pray. Each night and

day we sing and pray, _____ to thee we

pray, Lord to thee in hope we sing and

pray   To thee each night ____ and

day,   To thee we sing _____ and

pray;   Lord,   to thee   each

night   and day,   Strong   in hope   we

ad lib.

sing _____ and pray, we sing and pray;   strong   in

p

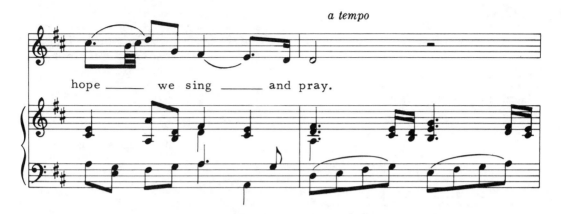

hope _____ we sing _____ and pray.

OLD LOVESONG

High key

From the Locheimer Liederbuch (1460)
Arranged by Royal Stanton

1. My thoughts by day, my dreams at night, are all of thee; My cho-sen love, my sole de-light, be true to me! Come, come, and bring thy love to charm me! Like a shield it guards my heart; No pow'r on earth can harm me.

2. My cho-sen love, my sole de-light, Hear what I sing: My heart, my life, and all I own to thee I bring. Thine, thine am I to-day, to-mor-row; Come what may, I vow to thee My love in joy or sor-row.

OLD LOVESONG

Low key

From the Locheimer Liederbuch *(1460)*
Arranged by Royal Stanton

For lowest voices, read this in E♭.

Gently (♩=72–84)

1. My thoughts by day, my
2. My cho-sen love, my

dreams at night are all of thee; My cho-sen love, my sole de-light, be
sole de-light, Hear what I sing: My heart, my life, and all I own to

true to me! Come, come, and bring thy love to charm me!
thee I bring; Thine, thine am I to-day, to-mor-row;

Like a shield it guards my heart; No pow'r on earth can harm me.
Come what may, I vow to thee My love in joy or sor-row.

O LORD MOST HOLY *(Panis Angelicus)*

César Franck

O Lord most ho - ly, O Lord al -
Pa - nis an - ge - li - cus fit pa - nis

might — y Fa - ther com - pas - sionate, we
ho - mi - num, Dat pa - nis coe - li - cus fi -

bring to thee our praise. _____ Help us to
gu - ris ter - mi - num; _____ O res mi -

know thee,   know   thee and   love — thee
ra - bi -lis   man -   du - cat   Do-mi-num

Fa -   ther,   Fa -   ther,   grant us thy truth   and
Pau -   per,   Pau -   per,   ser - vus et hu -   mi-

grace; ——   Fa -   ther,   Fa -   ther,
lis; ——   Pau -   per,   Pau -   per,

guide and de-fend —— us.
ser - vus et hu - mi - lis.

Rule in our will-ful hearts,
Pa - nis an - gel-i-cus

Guide thou our wand'ring thoughts.
fit pa - nis ho - mi - num,
In all our
Dat pa - nis

sor - rows let us find our rest in thee;
coe - li - cus fi - gu - ris ter - mi - num,

And in temp - ta-tion's hour,
O res mi - ra - bi - lis
Save by thy
man - du - cat

might-y power;   Thy _____ help _ send _ us;   Hear
Do-mi-num,   Pau _____ per, _ Pau _ per,   ser-

___ us in mer _ cy.   Show _____ thy _
___ vus et hu - mi - lis;   Pau _____ per,

fav _ or, So _____ we _ live and sing praise _____ to
Pau _ per, ser _ vus, ser-vus et hu _____ mi

thee!
lis.

SEBBEN, CRUDELE

Antonio Caldara

Lyrics (verse 1):
Seb-ben, cru - de - le, mi fai—lan - guir,— sem-pre fe-
Tho' not de - serv - ing Thy cru - el scorn,— Ev - er un-

de - le, sem-pre fe - de - le ti vo-glio a - mar.
swerv - ing, ev - er un - swerving Thee on - ly I— love.

Sebben, cru - de - le,
Tho' not de - serv - ing

mi fai lan - guir, —— sempre—fe - de - le ti— vo-glio a-
Thy cru - el scorn, —— Ev - er - un - swerv-ing Thee on - ly I

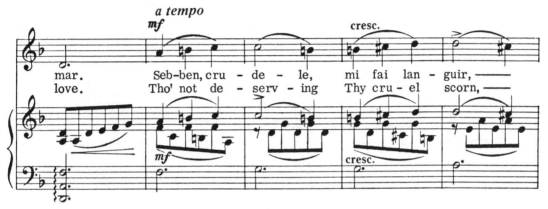

mar. Seb-ben, cru - de - le, mi fai lan - guir, ——
love. Tho' not de - serv - ing Thy cru - el scorn, ——

sem-pre fe - de - le ti- vo-glio a - mar. Con la lun -
Ev - er - un - swerv-ing Thee on - ly I love. When to thee

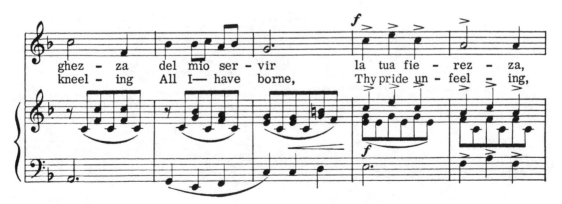

ghez - za del mio ser - vir la tua fie - rez - za,
kneel - ing All I— have borne, Thy pride un - feel - ing,

la tua fie - rez - za sa-prò stan - car, la tua fie -
Thy pride un - feel - ing I—then shall move, Thy pride un -

rez - za sa-prò stan - car.
feel - ing I—then shall move.

Seb-ben, cru - de - le, mi fai—lan - guir,
Tho' not de - serv - ing Thy cru - el scorn,

sem-pre fe - de - le, sem-pre fe - de-le ti vo-glio a-
Ev - er un - swerv - ing, ev - er un - swerving Thee on—ly I

mar.
love.

a tempo

Seb-ben, cru-
Tho' not de-

de - le, mi fai lan - guir,——— sempre fe - de - le ti—
serv - ing Thy cru - el scorn,——— Ev - er un - swerv-ing Thee

vo - glio a - mar, sebben, cru - de - le, mi fai lan -
on - ly I love, Tho' not de - serv - ing thy cru - el

guir,——— sempre fe - de - le ti - vo-glio a - mar.———
scorn,——— Ev-er un - swerving Thee on - ly I love.———

THE SILVER SWAN

High key

Orlando Gibbons
Solo adaptation by Royal Stanton

The sil - ver swan, who,

liv - ing, had no note, When death ap-proach'd, un - lock'd her si - lent

throat; Lean - ing her breast a - gainst the reed - y

shore, Thus sang her first and last, and sang no more:

"Fare-well all joys, O death, come close mine eyes; More

geese than swans now live, more fools than wise!"

THE SILVER SWAN

Low key

Orlando Gibbons
Solo adaptation by Royal Stanton

shore,   Thus sang her first and   last, and_ sang   no more:

"Fare - well all   joys,   O   death, come close   mine eyes;   More

geese than swans now   live, more_ fools   than wise!"

TAKE MY HEART

High key

Orlando di Lasso
Setting by Royal Stanton

Take my____ heart in - to____ your____ care, And soothe its sor - row and com -

plain - ing; Or, once a - gain be - fore____ we____ part, Ah! Hold me fast!

Hold___ me fast! Hold_____ me fast!

My lips that al - ways met___ you smil - ing, That spoke sweet words in -

to your ear, smile, a - las, no more, but are curs-ing, curs-ing those who drove me from you!

TAKE MY HEART

Low key

Orlando di Lasso
Setting by Royal Stanton

Take my____ heart in - to____ your____ care, And soothe its sor - row and com-

plain - ing; Or, once a - gain be - fore we part, Ah! Hold me fast!

Hold___ me fast! Hold_____ me fast!

faster (♩ = 126)

mf

My lips that al - ways met you smil - ing, That spoke sweet words in -

mp

cresc.

rit.

D. S. al fine

f

to your ear, Smile, a - las, no more, but are curs-ing, curs-ing those who drove me from you!

TO MUSIC *(An die Musik)*

High key
English words
by Royal Stanton

Franz Schubert

Moderato

Oh love - ly
Du hol - de

Art, when gloom - y hours I'm spend-ing, Or when I'm
Kunst, in wie - viel grau - en Stun - den, Wo mich des

torn by bit - ter storms of life, You warm my
Le - bens wil - der Kreis um - strickt, Hast du mein

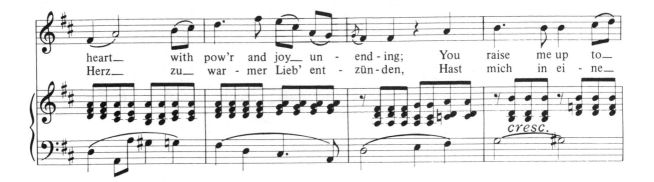

heart___ with pow'r and joy___ un - end - ing; You raise me up to___
Herz___ zu war - mer Lieb' ent - zün - den, Hast mich in ei - ne___

cresc.

realms un-known to strife, To bet-ter realms___ un-known___ to strife.
bess - 're Welt ent - rückt, in ei - ne bess - 're Welt___ ent - rückt.

p

You calm my
Oft hat ein

fp *fp* *pp*

sighs with tones of joy - ful___ sing - ing; On your sweet
Seuf - zer, dei - ner Harf' ent - flos - sen, Ein süs - ser

sounds my soul to heav'n can soar;
hei - li - ger Ak - kord von dir,

To - mor - row's
den Him - mel

skies will sound in joy - ous ring - ing; Oh love - ly Art, my
bess - 'rer Zei - ten mir er - schlos - sen, du hol - de Kunst, ich

cresc.

thanks, my thanks there - fore, Oh love - ly Art, — my thanks there - fore!
dan - ke dir da - für, du hol - de Kunst, ich dan - ke dir!

p

fp *fp*

TO MUSIC *(An die Musik)*

Low key
English words
by Royal Stanton

Franz Schubert

Moderato

Oh love - ly
Du hol - de

Art, when gloom - y hours I'm spend - ing,
Kunst, in wie - viel grau - en Stun - den,

Or when I'm
Wo mich des

torn by bit - ter storms of life,
Le - bens wil - der Kreis um - strickt,

You warm my
Hast du mein

heart___ with__ pow'r and joy__ un - end - ing; You raise me up to__
Herz___ zu__ war - mer Lieb' ent - zün - den, Hast mich in ei - ne__

realms un-known to strife, To bet-ter realms__ un-known__ to strife.
bess - 're Welt ent - rückt, in ei - ne bess - 're Welt___ ent - rückt.

You calm my
Oft hat ein

sighs with tones of joy - ful__ sing - ing; On your sweet
Seuf - zer, dei - ner Harf' ent - flos - sen, Ein süs - ser

sounds my soul to heav'n can soar;
hei - li - ger Ak - kord von dir,

To - mor - row's
den Him - mel

skies will sound in joy - ous ring - ing;
bess - 'rer Zei - ten mir er - schlos - sen,

Oh love - ly Art, my
du hol - de Kunst, ich

thanks, my thanks there - fore;
dan - ke dir da - für,

Oh love-ly Art my thanks there-fore!
du hol - de Kunst, ich dan - ke dir!

WHERE'ER YOU WALK

G. F. Handel
From Semele

Wher-e'er you walk, cool

gales shall fan the glade; Trees, where you sit, shall

crowd in-to a shade, trees, where you sit, shall crowd in-

to _____ a shade;

cresc.

Wher- e'er you walk, cool gales shall fan the glade;

Trees, where you sit, shall crowd in-to a_ shade, _____

r

trees, where you_ sit,

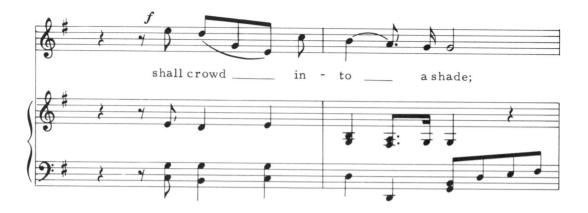

shall crowd _____ in - to _____ a shade;

Wher - e'er you tread, the

blush - ing flow'rs shall rise; And

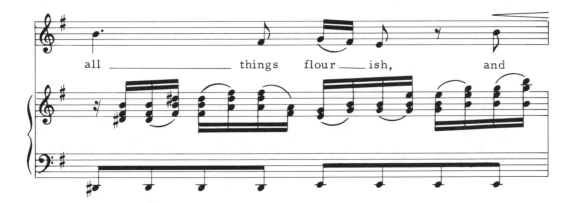

all _____ things flour___ish, and

all _____ things flour___ish wher-

e'er you turn your eyes, wher-

e'er you turn your eyes, where-e'er you turn your eyes.

WITH THEE THE DESOLATE MOOR

High key

G. F. Handel
From Solomon

With thee the des-o-late moor I'd —— tread, Nor

once of Fate com-plain; Though burn-ing suns flash round my ——

head, and cleave the bar-ren plain. Thy love ——ly

246

CONCERT SONGS

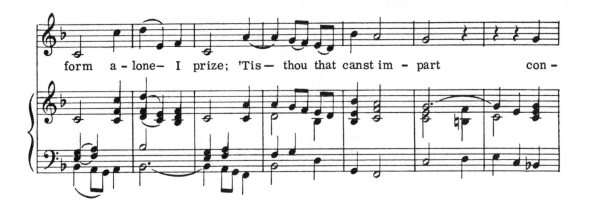

form a - lone— I prize; 'Tis— thou that canst im - part con -

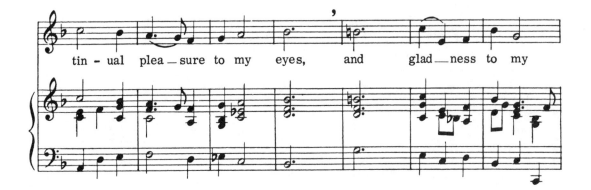

tin - ual plea - sure to my eyes, and glad - ness to my

heart; Con - tin - ual plea - sure to my eyes, and

glad - ness to— my heart.

rit.

WITH THEE THE DESOLATE MOOR

Low key

G. F. Handel
From Solomon

With thee the__ des - o-late moor I'd_____ tread,

Nor once of Fate com - plain; Though burn - ing__ suns flash

round my_____ head, and cleave the bar-ren plain. Thy

love - ly form a - lone_ I prize; 'Tis___ thou that canst im - part

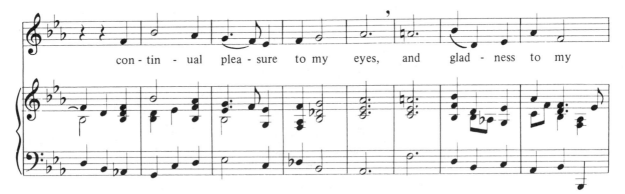

con - tin - ual plea - sure to my eyes, and glad - ness to my

heart; Con - tin - ual plea - sure to my_ eyes, and

glad - ness to_ my heart.

rit.

YOU FILL MY HEART *(Wie bist du, meine Königin)*

German text by H. von Daumer
English words by Royal Stanton

Johannes Brahms

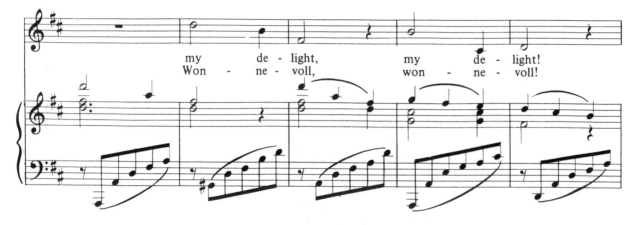

Text used by permission of Hinshaw Music, Inc., P.O. Box 470, Chapel Hill, NC 27514.

What love - ly
Frisch auf - ge -

prize can I com-pare to this de - light you grant___ my heart?
blüh - ter Ros-en Glanz, ver-gleich ich ihn dem dein - i - gen?

All oth - er joys so quick-ly fade be-fore its rap - ture!
Ach, ü - ber al - les, was da blüht, ist dei - ne Blü - te;

My de - light, my de - light!
Won - ne-voll, won - ne-voll!

Were you to walk on des-ert
Durch to - te Wü - stern wan-dle

sands,   cool shad-ows   green would go be - fore you;   Though hot bleak
hin,   und grü - ne Schat - ten breit-en   sich,____   ob fürch-ter-

winds   were blow-ing by,   I____   would not   heed   them.
lich - e Schwü-le dort   ohn   En - de   bru - te,

Ah,   my love!   You   are   my   de - light!
Won - ne - voll!   won - ne,   won - ne - voll!

Folksongs

AMERICA

Henry Carey

My coun-try, 'tis of thee, Sweet land of li - ber-ty, Of thee I

sing; Land where my fa - thers died, Land of the Pil-grim's pride,

From ev —'ry— moun-tain-side Let—Free-dom ring!

ALL THROUGH THE NIGHT

Welsh Folksong

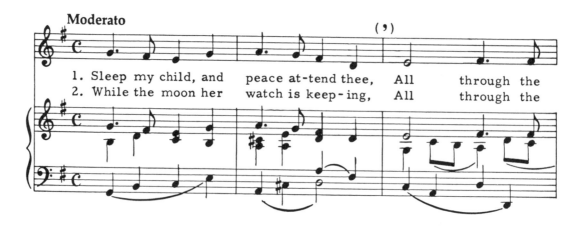

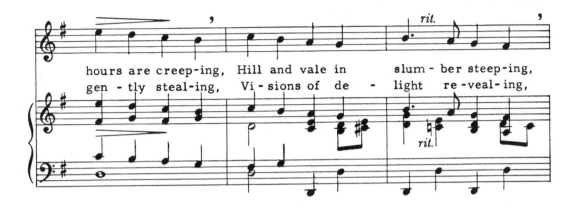

hours are creep-ing, Hill and vale in slum - ber steep-ing,
gen - tly steal-ing, Vi - sions of de - light re-veal-ing,

I my lov-ing vig - il keep-ing, All through the night.
Breathes a pure and ho - ly feel-ing, All through the night.

AULD LANG SYNE

Scottish Song

Should auld ac-quaint-ance be for-got, and

nev - er brought to mind? Should auld ac-quaint-ance

be for-got, and days of auld lang syne? For

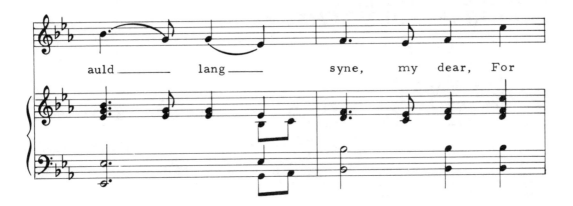

auld_____ lang_____ syne, my dear, For

auld_____ lang_____ syne; We'll take a cup o'

kind - ness yet, For auld_____ lang_____ syne!

BELIEVE ME, IF ALL THOSE ENDEARING YOUNG CHARMS

Moderato (♪=92)

Be— lieve me, if all those en - dear-ing young charms, which I

gaze on so fond - ly to - day,_____ Were to

change by to - mor- row and fleet in my arms like

fair - y gifts fa - ding a - way. _____ Thou wouldst

still be a - dored as this mo - ment thou art, Let thy

love - li - ness fade as it will; _____ And a -

rall.   *ten.*

round the dear ru - in each wish of my heart Would en -

twine it - self ver - dant - ly still. _____

BLACK IS THE COLOR

High key

Appalachian Folksong
Arranged by Royal Stanton

Black, black, black _____ is the col-or of my true love's hair, _____ Her/His lips _____ are some-thing won-drous fair; _____ The_pur - est_ eyes, and the dain - tiest_/strong-est_ hands; I love _____ the grass on where she/he stands; Black is the col-or of my true love's hair.

I

love my love and well $^{she}_{he}$ knows; _____ I love _____

_____ the ground on where $^{she}_{he}$ goes, _____ If $^{she}_{he}$ on earth no more I'd see, My

life _____ would quick-ly fade a-way; Black is the col-or of my true love's hair!

rubato

Black is the col-or of my true love's _____ hair! _____

colla voce

l.h.

BLACK IS THE COLOR

Low key

Appalachian Folksong
Arranged by Royal Stanton

Gently, in a reflective mood (♩ = 64)

Black, black, black_____ is the col-or of my

true love's hair,_____ Her / His lips_____ are some-thing won-drous fair;_____ The pur - est_____

eyes and the dain - tiest / strong-est__ hands; I love_____ the grass on where she / he stands;

Black is the col-or of my true love's hair. I

love my_ love and well ^{she}/_{he} knows_____ I love_____

_ the ground on where ^{she}/_{he} goes;___ If_ ^{she}/_{he} on earth no_ more_ I'd_ see, My

life——— would quick-ly fade a-way;___ Black is the col-or of my true love's hair!

Black is the col-or of my true love's_ hair!_____

O DEAR! WHAT CAN THE MATTER BE?

Old English Song
Setting by Royal Stanton

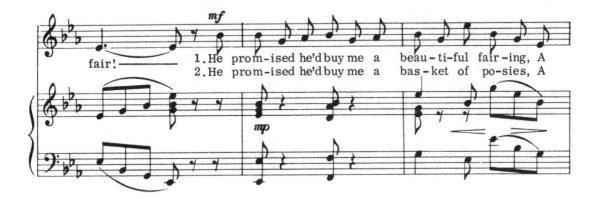

1. He prom-ised he'd buy me a beau-ti-ful fair-ing, A
2. He prom-ised he'd buy me a bas-ket of po-sies, A

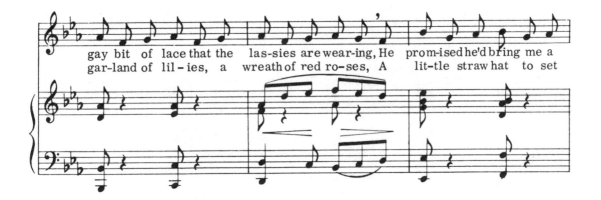

gay bit of lace that the las-sies are wear-ing, He prom-ised he'd bring me a
gar-land of lil-ies, a wreath of red ro-ses, A lit-tle straw hat to set

D.S. first time

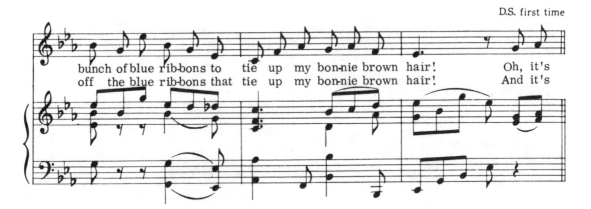

bunch of blue rib-bons to tie up my bon-nie brown hair! Oh, it's
off the blue rib-bons that tie up my bon-nie brown hair! And it's

Second time

O! Dear! What can the mat-ter be? Dear! Dear!

What can the mat-ter be? Oh! Dear! What can the mat-ter be?

John-ny's so long at the fair! ——— So long at the

fair! ——— So long at the fair! ———

John-ny's so long ——— at the fair!

DOWN IN THE VALLEY

American Folksong

1. Down in the val - ley, the val - ley so
   Hear the wind blow, dear, O hear the wind
2. Write me a let - ter con - tain - ing three
   Will you be mine, dear, O will you be

low, _____ Hang your head o -
blow! _____ Hang your head o -
lines; _____ An - swer my ques -
mine? _____ An - swer my ques -

ver, hear the wind blow! _____
ver, hear the wind blow! _____
tion: Will you be mine? _____
tion: Will you be mine? _____

DRINK TO ME ONLY WITH THINE EYES

High key
Ben Jonson

Old English Song

Drink to me on-ly with thine eyes, and I will pledge with mine;

Or leave a kiss with-in the cup and I'll not ask for wine. The

thirst that from the soul doth rise doth ask a drink di-vine;

But might I of Jove's nec-tar sup, I would not change for thine.

I sent thee late a ro - sy wreath, Not so— much hon - 'ring thee———

As giv-ing it a hope— that there— it could— not with - er'd be.——— But

thou— there-on didst on - ly breathe, And send'st it back— to me,———

Since when it grows, and smells,— I swear,— Not of— it-self, but thee!———

DRINK TO ME ONLY WITH THINE EYES

Low key
Ben Jonson

Drink to me on – ly with-thine eyes, And I–will pledge with mine;—

Or leave a kiss with – in—— the cup—and I'll—not ask for wine.—— The

thirst—that from the soul—doth rise doth ask a drink di – vine—

But might I of Jove's nec—tar sup,—I would not change for thine.

I sent thee late a ro— sy wreath, Not so— much hon'ring thee ———

As giv-ing it a hope that there— it could not with-'red be; ——— But

thou-there-on didst on — ly breathe, And send'st it back— to me ———

rit. *rit.*

Since when it grows, and smells, I swear, Not of— it-self, but thee! ———

rit. *rit.*

DU, DU!

German Folksong

1. You, you bring my heart glad-ness, You, you make my days bright;
2. Come, come, let's all be sing-ing, Come, come, let's all be glad;

(German) Du, du, liegst mir am Herz-en, Du, du, liegst mir im Sinn!

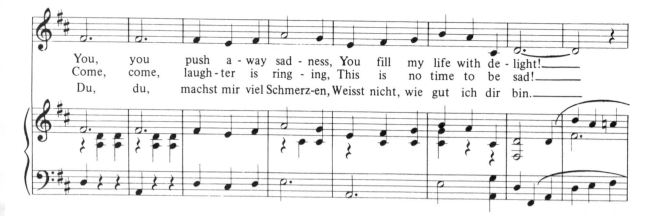

You, you push a-way sad-ness, You fill my life with de-light!
Come, come, laugh-ter is ring-ing, This is no time to be sad!
Du, du, machst mir viel Schmerz-en, Weisst nicht, wie gut ich dir bin.

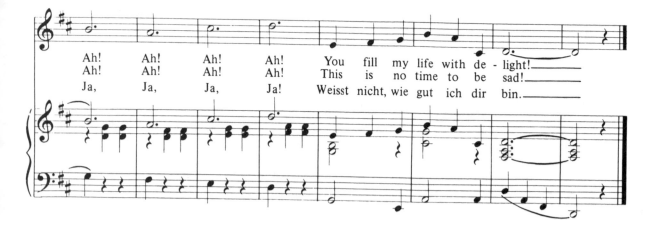

Ah! Ah! Ah! Ah! You fill my life with de-light!
Ah! Ah! Ah! Ah! This is no time to be sad!
Ja, Ja, Ja, Ja! Weisst nicht, wie gut ich dir bin.

274

GO DOWN, MOSES

American Spiritual

1. When Is-rael was in E-gypt's land; Let my peo-ple go!_____ Op-
2. Thus saith the Lord, bold Mo-ses said: Let my peo-ple go!_____ If
3. No more shall they in bond-age toil; Let my peo-ple go!_____ Let

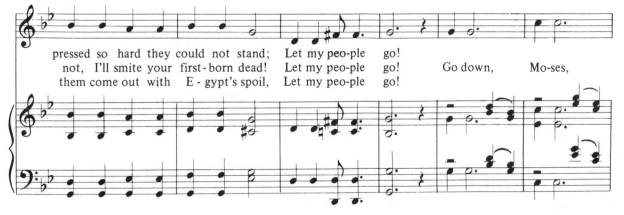

pressed so hard they could not stand; Let my peo-ple go!
not, I'll smite your first-born dead! Let my peo-ple go! Go down, Mo-ses,
them come out with E-gypt's spoil, Let my peo-ple go!

Way down in E-gypt's land. Tell old Phar-aoh,___ Let my peo-ple go!_____

HE'S GOIN' AWAY

High key

Southern American Mountain Song
Arranged by Royal Stanton

1. I'm goin' a-way for to stay a lit-tle while, But I'm
2. He's goin' a-way for to stay a lit-tle while, But he's

com-in' back, if I go ten thou-sand miles. Oh,
com-in' back, if he goes ten thou-sand miles. Oh,

who will tie your shoes? And who will glove your hand? And
pap - py'll tie my shoes, And mam - my'll glove my hand, And

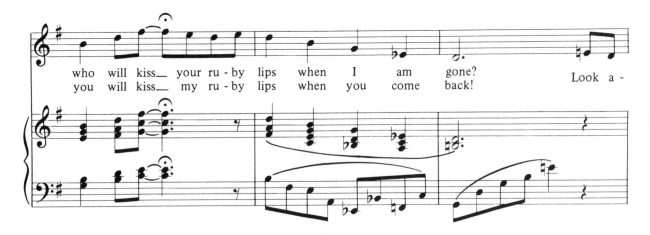

who will kiss___ your ru - by lips when I am gone? Look a -
you will kiss___ my ru - by lips when you come back! Look a -

way, Look a - way, Look a - way o - ver Yan - dro!

HE'S GOIN' AWAY

Low key

Southern American Mountain Song
Arranged by Royal Stanton

With great freedom (♪*always remains the same*)

1. I'm goin' a - way for to stay a
2. He's goin' a - way for to stay a

lit - tle while, _____ But I'm comin' back, if I
lit - tle while, _____ But he's comin' back, if he

go ten thou - sand miles. Oh,
goes ten thou - sand miles. Oh,

who will tie your shoes? And who will glove your
pap-py 'll tie my shoes, And mam-my'll glove my

hand? And who will kiss your ru - by
hand, And you will kiss my ru - by

lips when I am gone? _____ Look a - way, Look a -
lips when you come back! _____ Look a - way o - ver Yan-dro.

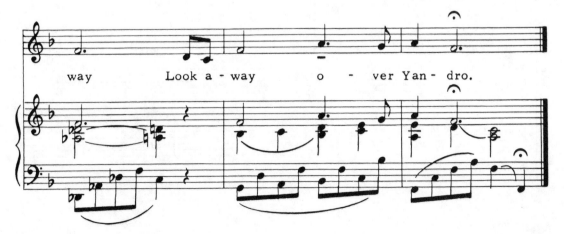

way Look a - way o - ver Yan - dro.

ON TOP OF OLD SMOKY

American Folksong

1. On top of old Smok - y, all cov - ered with snow _____ I lost my true lov - er by
2. A - court - in's a pleas - ure, a - part - ing is grief _____ A false-heart - ed lov - er is
3. A thief will but rob you of all that you save _____ But a false-heart - ed lov - er will
4. He'll hug you and kiss you and tell you more lies _____ Than cross ties on a rail - road, or

court - in'   too   slow.
worse than   a   thief.
send   you   to   grave.
stars   in   the   skies.

POOR WAYFARIN' STRANGER

High key
Arranged by Royal Stanton

American Folksong

I am a poor way-far-in' strang-er, A-trav-'ling through this world of woe; But there's no sick - ness, toil, or dan-ger In that bright world to which I go. I'm go-in' there to see my fath-er,/moth-er,/sis-ter,/broth-er, I'm go-in' there no more to roam! I'm just a - go - in' o-ver Jor-dan, I'm just a - go - in' o-ver home.

FOLKSONGS

POOR WAYFARIN' STRANGER

Low key
Arranged by Royal Stanton

American Folksong

THE TURTLE DOVE

High key

Folksong
Arranged by Royal Stanton

miles, my dear, though I go ten thou-sand miles.
thee, my dear, as— I will do for thee.

The— sea will nev-er run dry, my— dear, Nor the rocks nev-er melt in the
The— hills shall fly,— my tur-tle— dove, And the snow-capp'd moun-tains—

sun, And I nev-er will prove false to the one I— love, Till— all these things be
burn, Be-fore I prove false to the one I— love, Or— I a trai-tor

done, my dear, Till— all these things be done!
turn, my dear, Or— I a trai-tor turn!

THE TURTLE DOVE

Low key

Folksong
Arranged by Royal Stanton

well,__ my dear, I must be__ gone, And__ leave you__ for a__ while; But__
yon-der doth sit the tur-tle__ dove; He doth sit on__ yon-der high tree, A__

though I__ roam, I'll__ come back a-gain, though I go ten thou-sand
mak-ing a moan for the loss of his love, as__ I will do for

miles, my dear, though I go ten thou - sand miles.
thee, my dear, as — I will do for thee.

The— sea will nev-er run dry, my— dear, Nor the rocks nev-er melt in the
The— hills shall fly,— my tur - tle— dove, And the snow - capp'd moun-tains—

sun, And I nev-er will prove false to the one I— love, Till— all these things be
burn, Be - fore— I prove false to the one I— love, Or— I a trai - tor

done, my dear, Till— all these things be done!
turn, my dear, Or— I a trai - tor turn!

WHEN LOVE IS KIND

Traditional

1. When Love is kind,_____ cheer-ful and free,_____ Love's sure to
2. If Love can sigh_____ for one a - lone,_____ Well pleased am
3. Love must, in short,_____ keep fond and true,_____ Through good re -

find_____ wel-come from me; But when Love brings_____ heart-ache and
I_____ to be that one; But should I see_____ Love giv'n to
port_____ and e - vil too; Else here I swear,_____ young Love may

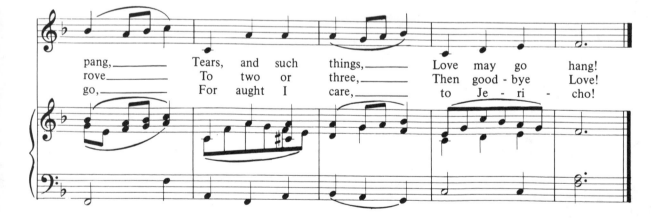

pang,_____ Tears, and such things,_____ Love may go hang!
rove_____ To two or three,_____ Then good - bye Love!
go,_____ For aught I care,_____ to Je - ri - cho!

Rounds

O HOW LOVELY IS THE EVENING

Three-Part Round: Divide into three groups, each group beginning as indicated by the numbers. May be sung as a trio, one person on a part.

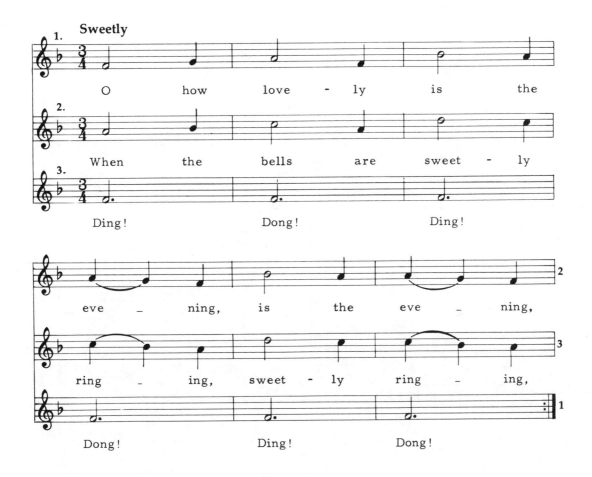

COMBINATION ROUND:
ARE YOU SLEEPING?
and THREE BLIND MICE

Rounds may be sung separately or together.

1.
Are you sleep - ing? Are you sleep - ing?
Three blind mice, three blind mice,

2.
Broth - er John! Broth - er John!
See how they run! See how they run!_____ They

3.
Morn-ing bells are ring - ing, Morn - ing bells are ring - ing,
all ran af-ter the farm - er's wife, she cut off their tails with a carv - ing knife, You

4.
Ding, ding, dong! Ding, ding, dong!
nev - er saw such a sight in your life As three blind mice.

DONA NOBIS PACEM